WOMEN IN SOCIETY

INDIA

VIJAYA GHOSE

MARSHALL CAVENDISH
New York • London • Sydney

Reference edition published 1994 by
Marshall Cavendish Corporation
2415 Jerusalem Avenue
P.O. Box 587
North Bellmore
New York 11710

© Times Editions Pte Ltd 1994

Originated and designed by
Times Books International, an imprint of
Times Editions Pte Ltd

Printed in Malaysia

Library of Congress Cataloging-in-Publication Data:
Ghose, Vijaya.
    Women in society. India / Vijaya Ghose. — Reference ed.
    p. cm.
    Includes bibliographical references and index.
    ISBN 1-85435-559-7 (set). — ISBN 1-85435-564-3 (volume)
    1. Women—India—Juvenile literature. 2. Women—India—
Social conditions—Juvenile literature. (1. Women—India.
2. India—Social conditions.) I. Title.
HQ1742.G48 1994
305.42'0954—dc20   93–46880
                      CIP
                       AC

Women in Society
Editorial Director	Shirley Hew
Managing Editor	Shova Loh
Editors	Michael Spilling
	Falak Kagda
	Roseline Lum
	Sue Sismondo
	MaryLee Knowlton
Picture Editor	Mee-Yee Lee
	Vijaya Ghose
Production	Edmund Lam
Design	Tuck Loong
	Ronn Yeo
	Felicia Wong
	Loo Chuan Ming
Illustrators	Anuar bin Abdul Rahim
	Eric Chew
	Atanu Roy
	William Sim
MCC Editorial Director	Evelyn M. Fazio
MCC Production Manager	Ruth Toda

Introduction

Myth, legend, and Hinduism give Indian women an exalted position. The goddess Durga, who slew the evil demon Mahisasura who was wreaking havoc on Earth when none of the gods could vanquish him, is the embodiment of *Shakti* ("SHEHK-ti") or power incarnate. Life-giving rivers like the Ganges and the Saraswati are believed to flow from goddesses.

Over the centuries, however, real women lost out to men. The reasons are partly historical. As marauders swept into India from the north, women took to the veil to hide from lustful eyes. Child marriage became, and still is, an accepted practice.

A woman in India has no identity besides that of some man's daughter, wife, mother, or grandmother. In very traditional homes, a husband addresses his wife as the mother of his son. For instance, the husband will say, "Oh, Ramu's mother, rub my legs." She is never referred to as the daughter's mother.

It was Mahatma Gandhi who gave women the position they deserve. During the 1940s freedom movement, Gandhi called on the women of India to fight along with the men. Some of India's most prominent women came to public attention during that time.

Women in Society India explores the changes that are slowly blowing away years of prejudice, particularly against the female child who is a second-class citizen from the moment of birth. But eliminating discrimination is a long and arduous fight. Thousands of years of prejudice are hard to change, but there is a glimmer of a beginning.

Contents

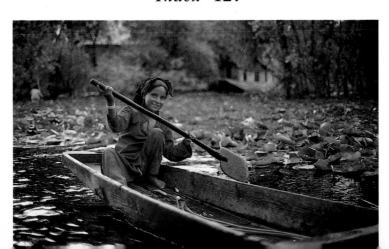

chapter one

Savitri

M yth and legend in India are not confined to books—they are very much a part of everyday life. In India, women have been and often still are dependent on men. But from time to time there have been women who got what they wanted through determination, grit, cunning, and perseverance.

In Indian mythology, five women—Sita, Savitri, Draupadi, Ahalya, and Arundhati—are held up as role models. They are known as the *pancha satis* ("pehn-chah sah-tis"), the five ideal women. All men want their wives to be like Sita: quiet, long-suffering, and obedient. Savitri's husband owed his life to her, and she got what is valued by Indian society—the status of a married woman. Draupadi is admired for her guidance of her five husbands, and Ahalya and Arundhati are revered for their steadfastness and fidelity.

The woman who outwitted the gods

Savitri, the daughter of King Aswapati, had grown into a beautiful young woman and studied music, philosophy, and astronomy. When it was time for Savitri to be married, no prince would have her because she was so learned. So King Aswapati sent her on a trip through many kingdoms to choose a husband.

The princess makes her choice As Savitri's entourage was traveling through a forest, she saw a handsome young hermit. His face became imprinted on her mind. None of the princes she saw could compare to the handsome hermit.

Opposite: A scene depicting Krishna, the dancing god. A rich mythology has been woven around the Hindu pantheon of gods.

Right: A young woman offering Indian sweets on a festival day.

On the way home, Savitri stopped and asked for some water. Just then, the hermit came up and offered her water. Savitri lost her heart to him. She learned that he was Satyavan, son of King Dyumatsen of Shalwa. Though a prince, he was poor because a neighboring king had taken advantage of Dyumatsen's blindness and Satyavan's youth to usurp their kingdom.

When the sage Narada heard that Savitri had chosen Satyavan, he told her father, King Aswapati, that Satyavan had only one year left to live. This was because the long-childless King Dyumatsen had prayed to the gods for a child, and was answered with a cruel choice: he could have a stupid child who would live for 100 years or a son who was astonishingly clever but would die before he was 20. King Dyumatsen had chosen the latter.

Knowing this, Savitri married Satyavan, exchanged her royal ways for a life in the forest, and served her husband and his parents with great devotion.

The end approaches As the year came to an end, Savitri knew that Satyavan's days were numbered. One day, they went to the forest as usual to gather wood. Satyavan complained of a headache and fell asleep with his head in her lap. Soon Savitri saw a man who had the brilliance of the sun riding a black buffalo.

Savitri asked him who he was. The man said he was Yama, the god of death, and that he had come to take Satyavan away.

He took the "life" out of Satyavan, tied his body with a rope, and set off. Savitri followed so that she would know where Satyavan was being taken. She ran behind Yama, praising his sense of justice, kindness, and generosity. She also made it clear that when she died she would like to be with her husband.

So pleased was Yama with her devotion that he said he would grant her any three wishes. Savitri asked for the sight and kingdom of her parents-in-law to be restored. Both wishes were granted. Next she asked to be the mother of 100 sons. Without hesitation, she was granted that too.

Then Savitri asked, "How can I have even one son without a husband?"

Yama pleaded with her to ask for another boon but Savitri would not budge. "A promise is a promise," she reminded him. Yama had been outwitted. He restored Satyavan to life and blessed him with 400 years on Earth.

The ideal Indian woman

Savitri typifies the quintessential Indian woman. Her courage and determination are understated, but even Death bows before her power. Her story is one of *pativrata* ("peh-ti-vrah-tah")—selfless

In India, the ideal wife is one who will give up her comforts to please her husband, as this bride will find out.

The concept of *pativrata*

In India, the ideal wife is one who looks on her husband as her lord and master and will give up her happiness and comfort to please him. Such a woman is called a *pativrata*, a woman selflessly and steadfastly loyal to her husband.

Major myths invariably convey the message that good and faithful women can overcome impossible situations. A chaste wife's devotion is said to be powerful enough to help her husband triumph in battle, overcome nature, and even defy death. The epitome of *pativrata* is Sita, immortalized in the Hindu epic *Ramayana*.

Sita, daughter of King Janak, marries Rama, son of King Dasarath. A few days after their marriage, a palace intrigue results in Rama's exile. Sita lives in the forest with him and is a devoted and chaste wife. While Rama is out hunting one day, Ravana, the demon-king of Lanka, carries Sita off. Sita remains faithful to her husband, however, and strenuously resists Ravana's advances. Rama rescues Sita, but then subjects her to *agni pariksha* ("AHG-ni peh-RICK-shah")—ordeal by fire—to test her chastity. So great is her fidelity that the flames refuse to consume her. However, since the people still question her chastity, Rama (having regained his kingdom) banishes her to the forest.

As the enduring image of Indian womanhood, Sita represents chastity, purity, and complete faithfulness that does not waver through Rama's slights, distrust, and ultimate rejection. The *Ramayana* is responsible for popularizing and perpetuating the belief that women are the property of men and that their outstanding virtue is fidelity.

Surprisingly, this image of a long-suffering, obedient, and faithful wife is reinforced by women. Mothers teach their daughters that the ultimate joy in life is to be married. A woman is expected to treat her husband like a god and put up with insult and indignity for the sake of his happiness. Women, a girl is told, are subservient to men and she must accept that situation if she is to be happy.

Most women fall into the mold that society expects of them, which means that they don't work outside the home and are therefore economically dependent on their husbands. As a result, they endure all kinds of ill-treatment. But years of subjugation have taught Indian women to be survivors. Like Savitri, they have learned to manipulate situations to make the best of their circumstances.

devotion to her husband. Savitri personifies the clever and devoted wife. More so than the others of the *pancha satis*, it is Savitri, along with Sita, who has been the role model for Indian women down through the ages.

Women today

The lot of most Indian women today is similar to that of Savitri and Sita, with a slight difference. Modern-day Indian women put up with indignity and degradation from sheer economic necessity. Generally only slightly educated, not trained for any profession, and taught from childhood that a husband's word is law, most find it easier to suffer rather than leave the security of the home to look for a job to support themselves and their children. That is one reason for the low divorce rate in India.

There is the additional factor of societal pressure. Girls are taught by their mothers that their main purpose in life is to be a wife and mother, and they are groomed from an early age for these roles. Being a single woman in India—whether single from choice, divorce, or widowhood—is regarded as unnatural and often as bad luck and a disgrace to the family. This is still the prevailing attitude, even though India has had a woman prime minister, and a widowed one at that!

But times are changing. More and more girls are going to school, and more

and more women are working outside the home. As women begin to realize the power of literacy and economic independence, they are shedding their fears and fetters.

Modern young daredevils who earn a living by riding the "well of death."

chapter two

Milestones

ndia is a land of five major religions—Hinduism, Islam, Christianity, Jainism, and Buddhism. The majority of the people are Hindus, who have a caste system that has existed for thousands of years. This system divides people into classes. The four main castes are the Brahmin ("BRAH-min") or priestly caste; the Kshatriya ("SHAH-tri-yah") or warrior caste; the Vaisya ("VY-shah") or trader caste; and the Sudra ("SOOD-rah") caste, who do all the lowly jobs and because of it are considered untouchable.

A woman's position in society depends on her caste, class, community, language group, and religion. For instance, a traditional Muslim woman is expected to wear a *burqah* ("BUR-kah"), the heavy cape and veil that cover a woman from head to foot. A woman from a traditional Brahmin home moves about more freely than a Muslim woman, but only within the house. A Hindu woman of a lower caste not only moves about freely, but also earns a living outside the home.

The history of the position of women in India has fluctuated over the years—sometimes excellent and other times abominable. To understand women's status in Indian society today, we need to know what shaped attitudes toward women.

Opposite: A young girl working at a construction site. In poor families, all adults and children need to work in order to feed the family.

Right: A mother and her child in the marketplace.

Women in Vedic India

Historians say that the status of women was best in Vedic India (c. 1500 B.C.–A.D. 600), soon after the migration of the Aryans into the subcontinent. The Aryans were nature worshipers.

A statue of a goddess in a temple. In Vedic India, gods and goddesses were worshiped equally.

in the hymns of the *Rig Veda*, the first of the four philosophical texts of the Aryans. The Vedic goddess Usha is the precursor of the female deities of Hinduism.

The *Rig Veda* shows that women were treated equally with men in all spheres, including access to the highest knowledge. Though most of the hymns in the *Rig Veda* are by male *rishis* ("ree-shees"), or holy men, it also contains hymns by women.

In this liberal society, a woman participated in all religious rites along with her husband. Educated and accomplished women were given the highest social status.

Vedic society was patriarchal and believed in monogamy, or being married to one person at a time. Marriage, according to the *Rig Veda*, was a holy sacrament and could not be dissolved.

This is not to say that everything was ideal for women. There were instances of injustice toward women even on the part of the gods. In the Hindu epic *Ramayana*, for example, Rama makes Sita go through the *agni pariksha*, or ordeal by fire, to prove her chastity, and even after the flames refuse to consume her because of her fidelity, banishes her from his kingdom. (See Chapter 1.)

The Laws of Manu The *Manu Smriti* is a book from Vedic times of the laws that govern society. It is a collection of

They saw God in the world around them—in the sun, stars, moon, rivers, trees, and all living creatures. The pantheistic, or nature-worshiping, Aryans celebrated goddesses as well as gods.

The gods and goddesses of ancient India were symbols of the natural forces and especially of life and death. Indra is the god of the firmament and Usha, the beautiful dawn goddess, is celebrated beliefs and traditions compiled by various authors. It is attributed to Manu because *Manu* means the wise one and is also a generic term for human. The laws of Manu are particularly derogatory to women, although some of the finest sayings about women are also from Manu. This reflects the ambivalent attitude toward women that has been prevalent in India down through the ages—women are worshiped as goddesses but at the same time treated like slaves.

The philosophy expressed in the *Manu Smriti* can be likened to the symbolism of seed and the earth. Man provides the seed, the essence, for the creation of the offspring. This seed determines the child's identity. The role of the woman, like the earth, is simply to receive the seed and help it to grow. This implied that man was the lord, master, owner, and provider. A woman was seen as nothing more than a commodity or a possession.

"Women must be honored and adorned by their fathers, brothers, husbands, and brothers-in-law who desire great good fortune.

"Where women verily are honored, there the gods rejoice; where, however, they are not honored, there all sacred rites prove fruitless."

from Manu Smriti

Indian mythology further reflects this theme of the supreme man. The ideal women of Indian mythology are paragons of virtue and wifely devotion. Sita, Savitri, Draupadi, Ahalya, and others are portrayed as dutiful, truthful, chaste, and self-sacrificing women who are completely devoted to their husbands—the sort of wife every Indian man looks for.

"A woman must constantly worship her husband as a god, even though he is destitute of virtue or womanizes. A woman should be kept in dependency by her husband because by nature women are passionate and disloyal. Ideal women are those who do not strive to break these bonds of control. The salvation and happiness of women revolve around their virtue and chastity as daughters, wives, and widows."

from Manu Smriti

Women's status declines

The *Puranas* are a series of 18 books written by Brahmin scholars from about A.D. 200 to 1000. These books of mythology gave an exalted place to feminine deities, but reduced women in real life to the position of domestic slaves or playthings. This was in marked contrast to the spirit of the *Rig-vedic* verse chanted during the wedding ceremony.

From the *Rig-vedic* marriage verse

As the bride and groom take the seven steps, or *saptapadi* ("SEHP-tah-pah-thee"), symbolic of a joint journey through life, the groom says to the bride:

"Having taken seven steps with me, become my friend;

May we two, who have taken together these seven steps become companions;

May I have your friendship;

May I not be separated from your friendship, nor you from mine;

With utmost love to each other …

With mutually amicable minds, and enjoying together

Our food and invigorating things,

May we walk together and take our resolves together;

May our minds be united, of the same vows and thoughts;

I am the *rik* ("rick," text), you are the *saman* ("seh-MAHN," tune);

I am the *saman*, you are the *rik*."

In contrast to this, one of the most offensive passages in Puranic literature concerning women occurs in the *Padma Purana*, c. A.D. 750. It lays down the following rules for married women:

"There is no other god on earth for a woman than her husband. The most excellent of all the good works that she can do is to seek to please him by manifesting perfect obedience to him. Therein should lie her sole rule of life.

"Be her husband deformed, aged, infirm, offensive in his manners; let him also be choleric, debauched, immoral, a drunkard, a gambler; let him frequent places of ill-repute, live in open sin with other women, have no affection whatever for his home; let him rave like a lunatic; let him live without honor; let him be blind, deaf, dumb, or crippled; in a word, let his defects be what they may, let his wickedness be what it may, a wife should always look upon him as her god, should lavish on him all her attention and care, paying no heed whatsoever to his character and giving him no cause whatsoever for displeasure."

Since women were given the lowest status, as mere chattels to their husbands, they were also deemed unfit to be educated. Indian women of Puranic times put up with not merely the drudgery and indignity of their lives, but all the injustice inherent in their society—just as many women do today.

Jainism and Buddhism

The sixth century B.C. was a period of great intellectual and spiritual activity all over the world. It was also a time of intense social reform. This was the time of the early Greek philosophers and Hebrew prophets. Confucius in China and perhaps Zoroaster (founder of the Parsi religion) in Persia were expounding their philosophy.

In India, two new religions arose in protest against the orthodox early Hindu practices of Vedic India. Vardhamana Mahavira (599–527 B.C.) laid the foundations of Jainism, a religion dedicated to nonviolence. Prince Siddhartha Gautama (563–483 B.C.) gave up his kingdom in favor of meditation and learning and founded Buddhism. He is better known as the Buddha, meaning the Enlightened One. He was a contemporary of Mahavira. Neither was a Brahmin; both were born into warrior clans.

Both religions kept up the Vedic tradition of giving women an honored place in social life. The Jains had two monastic orders, ascetics and householders. Both orders were open to women as well as to Sudras (the lowest caste).

Jain nuns leaving after visiting the sacred temple at Palitana.

The Buddha had a high regard for women. He said to his favorite disciple, Ananda: "Women are competent. If they retire from household life to the homeless state under the doctrine and discipline (of Buddhism), they can attain sainthood."

The main principle of Jainism is *ahimsa* ("eh-HIM-sah"), or non-injury to all living creatures. Mahavira attracted many disciples; several of them were women.

Jains also made significant contributions in astronomy, logic, mathematics, and grammar. Jain women had access to this learning. A female Jain scholar of the seventh century, Yakini Mahattara, is said to have defeated a male Brahmin scholar, Haribhadra, in debate.

Buddhism also accorded women the respect they deserved. There was a Buddhist order of nuns, whereas women in Hinduism were left out of the higher religious orders.

Shantala, a Buddhist, was the wife of a 12th-century Hoysala ruler, Vishnu Vardhana (the Hoysalas were one of the dynasties that ruled South India). Her husband was so obsessed with war and acquisition of property that Shantala was left more or less to her own devices. Revolted by violence, she constantly urged her husband to desist from warring with other states. In his absence, she devoted herself to supervising temple building. One of the most beautiful temples she supervised is the Chenna Kesava temple at Belur. She is also believed to have built the water tank (reservoir) and garden at Sravanabelgola ("SREH-vah-nah-bay-lah-go-lah").

Shantala supervising the building of a temple.

Women in Buddhism

Among the women disciples of Buddha was Amrapali, originally a wealthy courtesan. She gave her mango grove with its buildings to the *sangha* ("SEHNG-hah"), or order of Buddhist monks.

Visakha was a laywoman who gave generously to the Buddhist cause and built a great monastery. The Buddha himself is said to have appreciated her hospitality and financial support, offered out of sheer religious devotion.

There is a famous story about Kissa Gautami, one of the leaders of Buddhist reformation. Distraught by the death of her child from snake-bite, she rushed to the Buddha and asked him to revive the baby. Buddha said he was willing to do so, provided she brought him something from a house never visited by death. He then gave her Enlightenment, and appointed her superintendent of the *sangha* at Jetavana, now in Uttar Pradesh.

Perhaps the first Buddhist woman missionary was Sanghamitra, daughter of Emperor Asoka. In the third century B.C. Sanghamitra, along with her brother Mahendra, led a mission to the island of Lanka (now Sri Lanka). It is said that this mission laid the foundation for the conversion of the people of the island to Buddhism.

The later teachers

Charaka was a famous Indian physician. Sushruta was a brilliant surgeon and is known as the first plastic surgeon. Both men lived and taught before the Christian era. Their teachings were systematized into standard texts by the fourth century.

Aryabhata, the fifth-century astronomer invented algebra. The seventh-century mathematician Brahmagupta expounded the laws governing *shunya* ("SHOON-yah"), or zero. Bhaskara, the 12th-century astronomer and mathematician, named his magnum opus *Lilavati* after his daughter. There is, however, some controversy surrounding *Lilavati*. While most accept it as Bhaskara's work, a certain group of researchers believes that *Lilavati* was written by a woman called Lilavati.

Alongside the pathbreakers in science, there were a succession of religious and social reformers in India.

In South India, a Tamil poet of the fifth century called Tiruvalluvar promoted his belief in "oneness with all."

Andal was a woman saint of the ninth century, the only woman among the 12 Tamil saint-poets known as Alwars. She and another poet, Nammalwar, hold the highest place among them in terms of literary merit. Her poems are in praise of Lord Krishna. Andal's verses in the *Tiruppavai* are widely sung in Tamil Nadu, especially by young women, to this day. She is the counterpart of North India's Mirabai, a great saint-poet of the 16th century (see page 88).

Around A.D. 1160, women writers of Karnataka, a city in South India, joined a new movement called Virashaivism (vi-rah-SHY-vi-zehm).

Though essentially religious, Virashaivism also included on its agenda reforms in social, political, and economic life. It was against the caste system, the priesthood, and idol worship. The *vachanas* ("veh-chah-nahs"), or sayings, of these women show that they believed every individual, irrespective of sex or social origin, could attain spiritual realization.

The Bhakti movement

The medieval Bhakti, or devotional, movement provided an outlet for economic and social discontent. It especially appealed to artisans and cultivators, who were ranked low in the Brahminical hierarchy. Bhakti philosophy was revolutionary for its time. A typical example are these lines of Basvanna, a famous Bhakti: "To the servant of God, who could eat if served, Hindus say 'go away,' but to the image of God, which cannot eat, they offer dishes of food."

One of the reasons for Bhakti poets' popularity was that they composed songs in local languages and not Sanskrit, the language of the upper classes.

Many of the poet-saints of this time were women. Because these women led such unconventional lives, they ran greater risk of social censure than men.

The mystic poems of Lalleswari

Lalleswari lived in the beautiful land of Kashmir in the 14th century. She was popularly known as Lal Ded and is revered as a saint by both Hindus and Muslims. She condemned idol worship. "An idol is but stone," she said, "and a temple is but stone." She was also against animal sacrifice. She called it folly to "offer a living sheep to a lifeless stone."

Her *vakh* ("VAHCK"), or sayings, have become a part of the repertoire of the village singer and the Sufi *kalam* ("kah-lum"), which is a spiritual song sung at the start of an assembly of Sufis or spiritual seekers.

There are many legends attached to Lal Ded's life. Once, a story goes, when she fetched water from the well, her husband hit the pitcher on her head with a stick. The pot broke, but the water remained frozen on her head. Later, it is said, she left her husband's home and wandered naked, singing songs and dancing in ecstasy. *Lalla-vakhyan*, a collection of her verses, is the oldest work in the Kashmiri language.

Islam comes to India

India has had long spells of Islamic rule. The first Muslim raids were between A.D. 999 and 1024. From then on, Islam continued to grow, reaching its peak in the Mughal Empire in the 16th century. The last of the Mughal emperors was deposed by the British in 1858.

Islam allowed men four wives and was strict with its women. Islam also preached brotherhood and equality and gave the right of inheritance to daughters, even if their share was less than that of sons. Under Islamic law, a son is entitled to inherit twice as much of his parents' estate as his sister. The rationale is that a man has to support his wife, while a woman will be supported by her husband, and so needs less.

The contribution of Emperor Akbar

Emperor Akbar (1542–1605) was the most noteworthy of the Mughals. He was tolerant of other religions and even married a Hindu woman. The tradition of Akbar's statesmanship and interest in all religions was continued by and large by his successors, Jahangir (reigned 1605–1627) and Shah Jahan (c. 1592–1666).

After that, the country went into decline politically. Shah Jahan's successor, Aurangzeb (1618–1707), was a fanatic who turned the Mughal Empire into an Islamic state.

Aurangzeb reinforced the *jiziya* ("jee-zee-yah"), the notorious poll-tax levied on Hindus. He began a policy of constant warfare in the South and the

The different faces of Muslim women: one in the traditional *burqah* (middle), one in a *burqah* but with just her head covered (right), and the third bare-headed.

The Taj Mahal was built by Mughal Emperor Shah Jahan as a mausoleum for his beloved wife Mumtaz Mahal.

North between Muslim kingdoms and the Marathas, Rajputs, and Sikhs, conflicts that made India vulnerable to British colonialists.

In these unsettled conditions, the Hindu and Muslim communities, once very interactive, grew apart. They became, in the words of Jawaharlal Nehru, India's first prime minister, "closed systems" with little interaction. Upper-caste Hindus became rigid in observing orthodox customs in order to preserve their identity. Priestcraft flourished, untouchability was rigorously observed, and child marriage enforced. The women of North India, even the Hindus, were kept in seclusion simply for security.

The rise of Sikhism

Sikhs are very distinctive people. They are tall and handsome and the men sport turbans and beards. Sikhism forbids the cutting of hair. Sikh women are among the loveliest in India, but like the men are fiercely militant when the need arises. Though a small community, Sikh contribution to public life has been enormous in the fields of defense, sports, agriculture, industry, and transportation.

The founder of Sikhism was Guru Nanak (1469–1539). Born into a non-Brahmin family, he preached the equality of humankind and rejected ideas of high and low classes based on sex, caste, or wealth.

The Sikh holy book, a compilation

known as the *Adi Granth*, includes a large selection from the saint-poet Kabir, other Hindu Bhaktas (adherents of the Bhakti movement), and Muslim Sufis. Their message was similar to Nanak's.

British rule

The British came to India to trade, through the East India Company, in the early part of the 17th century and stayed on to rule. By the middle of the 18th century, they were masters of virtually the entire subcontinent. The Mughal emperor in Delhi, once the sole ruler of the subcontinent, now continued merely as a figurehead.

Guru Nanak wanted women to be treated by men as equals: "Within a woman is a man conceived, from a woman is he born, he is married to a woman, and with her he goes through life. ... Why call her bad, who gives birth to kings? None may exist without a woman."

British rule brought about many painful changes. The imposition of the colonial economy had numerous adverse effects, not the least of which was the ruining of the renowned Indian weaving industry. However, British rule laid the foundation stone of formal education in India.

Sikh women at the Golden Temple in Amritsar.

Many of the reform movements of this time were inspired by religious fervor. The movements begun in the first half of the 19th century were the result of secular education, which encouraged rational and scientific thought.

The British were initially reluctant to introduce modern education, so some Indians learned English privately to gain access to the new scientific knowledge and political ideas of the West. Foremost among them was Raja Ram Mohun Roy (c. 1774–1833), who has been described as the Father of Modern Enlightenment in India. In 1828, Roy founded the Brahmo Samaj—Association of the Worshipers of God—which fought for reforms in religion, education, legal and political thought, and the status of women. He spoke out against *sati* ("sah-tee"), the practice of burning Hindu widows alive on their husbands' funeral pyres, and the ostracization of non-Hindu widows, and insisted that women should have the same rights and privileges as men. Roy was responsible for the gradual but sweeping changes that were marking Indian society.

Bengali pioneers

The women of Bengal were the first to take to education. As early as 1835 Bengali women wrote letters to journals asking for the spread of women's education. They also pressed for changes such as allowing widows to remarry.

Iswar Chandra Vidyasagar's campaign to legalize remarriage finally resulted in the Hindu Women's Remarriage Act in 1856. This act changed the status of widows by giving them the right to marry again and lead meaningful lives. Unfortunately, social convention and illiteracy—not being able to read about the act—prevented many women from taking advantage of this right.

Another social evil that women protested was the polygamy practiced by some classes. The Kulin Brahmins in Bengal, for example, had numerous wives, some of whom they never saw once the wedding ceremony was over. They married only for the sake of the dowry. After that the girl was left to fend for herself. Either she went back to her father's house, or if her husband took her to his home, she was treated like a slave. Many English-educated reformers attempted to put an end to this practice legally, but they were not successful. The act outlawing polygamy was finally passed after India wrested independence from the British.

The second half of the 19th century saw the birth of several reform movements throughout the country. These had a revolutionary impact on the lives of women. A major component of these reform movements was changing attitudes toward women. Women themselves were a target, to get them to change their attitudes toward themselves and toward other women.

Reforms in South India

Many prominent persons in the late 19th and early 20th centuries fought for rights for women, including women's right to education and inheritance and for widows to remarry, against child marriages and against untouchability—the ostracization of the Sudras.

Among women pioneers in the South was Venakamaba, a Telugu poet. Born early in the 19th century into an orthodox Brahmin family, she refused to have her head shaved, as was customary, along with a prohibition on wearing jewelry in order to be identified as a widow, when her husband died.

Opposite: A Rajasthani child bride. Although illegal, child marriages are still commonplace, especially in Rajasthan.

Rassundari's quest for learning

Rassundari (1809–1900) wrote *Amar Jiban* (My Life), in two parts. The first was published in 1868. She wrote the second half in the 1890s when she was over 80 years old. Unlike many who wrote later, Rassundari received little encouragement from her family. The wife of a prosperous East Bengal *zamindar* ("zeh-MIN-dahr"), or landowner, Rassundari recounts in her book how she used to hide pages removed from her son's books within the folds of her *sari*. When alone, she attempted to decipher what was written. She felt strongly about being denied education and reflected that "women were indeed unfortunate and could be counted as being animals." But "my mind would not accept this and was always restless with the urge to learn."

(Adapted from *Voices Within* by Dr. Malavika Karlekar)

A literacy class for women. Indian women are waking up to the power of literacy and education.

Reforms in West India

Jotirao Phule (1827–1890) took up the cause of women's education. Since there were no women teachers, he educated his wife. He opened a school for women of the lower castes in 1848 where he made his wife a teacher.

Gopal Ganesh Agarkar (1856–1895) started a Marathi (an Indian language) and English journal *Sudharak*, ("soo-dhah-rahk"), meaning reformer. The English columns were contributed by Gopal Krishna Gokhale (1866–1915), who later became Indian independence fighter Mahatma Gandhi's mentor. Both Agarkar and Gokhale campaigned strongly against untouchability. They worked actively for women's education and the remarriage of widows.

Ramabai Ranade (1862–1924) worked with her husband for women's education. She was active in the Seva Sadan in Bombay, an organization that trained women for educational and medical relief work. Branches of the organization were soon established in Ahmedabad, Surat, and Poona.

D.K. Karve (1858–1962), popularly known as Maharishi Karve, crusaded relentlessly against injustice to women. In 1891, he founded the Vidhava Vivaha Pratibandi Nivarak Mandali (Society for the Removal of Obstacles to the Remarriage of Widows). It was formed to help needy widows and to provide for their children's education.

First women's university When women's education was still in its infancy, Karve established a women's university for which he collected funds in England, the United States, and East Africa. Set up in Poona in 1916, it received a donation of $6,000 from Sir Vithaldas Thackersey. The university was named Shreemati Nathibai Damodar Thackersey (SNDT) Women's University in memory of Thackersey's mother.

SNDT University moved to Bombay in 1936, and since then many prominent Indian women have graduated from the university. What was remarkable about SNDT University was that courses were conducted in the Indian languages at a time when English was used for elementary teaching elsewhere. English, however, was taught as a compulsory subject at the university.

In Gujarat Vithalbhai Patel (1873–1933) introduced a bill in the Bombay Municipal Council to validate intercaste Hindu marriages. This failed as the Bombay Municipal Council was dissolved. It was only in 1949 that Prime Minister Nehru's parliament passed the Hindu Marriages Validity Act, which legalized intercaste marriages.

Vidyagauri Nilkanth (1876–1958) was a woman pioneer of Gujarat. She educated herself after marriage and became one of the first women graduates in the state. She founded the Mahila Mandal school in 1914 and the Lalshanker Umashankar College for Women, both in Ahmedabad. She was awarded the *Kaiser-i-Hind* medal by the British in 1926 for her outstanding work in the field of education, but she returned the award during the civil disobedience movement of 1930, which was part of the independence movement.

Dayanand Saraswati (1824–1883), taking his stand on the very Vedas invoked by Hinduism, campaigned against idol worship, untouchability,

In between classes at a women's college.

Today the Arya Samaj is a vast organization with a network of school spread all over the country.

The Ramakrishna Mission, a social serivce organization founded by Swami Vivekananda (1863–1902) in the second half of the 19th century, had many women members. Prominent among them was Margaret Elizabeth Noble (1867–1911), better known as Sister Nivedita, an Irish woman who settled in India and became a disciple of Swami Vivekananda. The Ramakrishna Mission has been called the Hindu version of Mother Teresa's Missionaries of Charity.

Reforms in the Muslim community

A parallel reform movement was also sweeping the Muslim community. The most notable Muslim reformer was Sir Syed Ahmed Khan (1817–98). He founded a school in 1875 that became the Aligarh Muslim University in 1921. The Muslim community had been slow in adopting modern English education. Syed Ahmed urged Muslims to come out of isolation and join the mainstream of society. He attacked the *purdah* ("PERH-dah") system, which kept women in complete seclusion from men who were not close relatives and required women to wear the *burqah* when outside the home. He challenged the prevailing idea that a Western education for women would result in women becoming wild and uncontrollable.

Wooden idols on sale. Dayanand Saraswati, who founded the Arya Samaj, discouraged idol worship as actively as he advocated women's rights.

child marriage, and the relegation of women to an inferior status. He advocated women's education, free choice of husband, and the right of every woman to study the Vedas. In 1875, he founded the Arya Samaj, an organization that fought for these principles. Set up to counter ritualism and dogmatism in the Hindu religion, the Arya Samaj was open to men and women alike. Many people choose to be married through the Arya Samaj rites, which emphasizes the responsibility of both spouses.

The emancipation of Indian Muslim women was a much slower process compared to that of other Indian women, partly because modern education entered the community later and partly because community leaders defended the *purdah* system. But although delayed and slow, education spread. It led to a decline in the practice of polygamy. Reformers also tried to revive widow remarriage, which had become taboo among the higher classes of Muslims, although not forbidden in Islam. The practice of denying inheritance to daughters, contrary to Islamic law, was also addressed.

These various strands of reform movements begun in the 19th century gained strength from the independence movement. From 1919, Gandhi's call for *swaraj* ("SWAH-rahj"), or independence, and social regeneration became two faces of the same coin.

Impact of the Sepoy Revolt

In 1857, the sepoys (British regiments of Indian soldiers) revolted at Meerut in Uttar Pradesh. The causes were many. Two concerns were the fact that Indian soldiers were not allowed to become officers and the British-implemented Doctrine of Lapse, which meant that any Indian kingdom without a male heir would automatically become the property of the British. But the spark setting off the revolt was a rumor that the cartridges the soldiers had to bite off before use were greased with fat from

Reforms in the Muslim community, in terms of education and liberalization, came slowly but they did come, giving Muslim women like these the freedom to go to school, work outside the home, and not wear the *burqah*.

beef and pork—Hindus do not eat beef as they believe the cow is a ed animal, while Muslims are forbidden to eat pork.

The revolt awakened nationalist fervor, and various regional "political consciousness" organizations were formed by the Indian intelligentsia. This led to a demand for an all-India forum, resulting in the formation of the Indian National Congress (INC). Its first

Mahatma Gandhi with Lord and Lady Mountbatten. Lord Mountbatten was the governor-general of India and India's independence had to be negotiated through him. Gandhi, India's freedom fighter who believed in peaceful protest, is more often referred to by his title Mahatma, meaning enlightened, than his given name, Mohandas Karamchand.

session was held in Bombay in 1885. Initially intended as a forum for discussion of important matters, the INC soon transformed itself into a political body to fight British authority.

Women's contribution The first four sessions of the INC record no women delegates. Then, in 1889, in the fifth session, Kadambini Ganguly, one of India's first women medical graduates, was enrolled as a member.

Within two decades women took part in the protest of the partition of Bengal, which was announced in July 1905. In all, 500 women participated. It was the first time that such a large number of women demonstrated their disapproval.

So successful was this agitation that women decided to get together to use the boycott of foreign goods as a political tool in the *swadeshi* ("SWAH-they-shee"), or national movement. They had realized that if they were to make any worthwhile contribution, their movement had to be political also. Women contributed their gold and jewelry for the promotion of the *swadeshi* movement. They made bonfires of foreign cloth in the open so that other women could see and boycott foreign goods.

By now women were slowly but surely making a very visible contribution to national resurgence. The Home Rule League was formed in 1916 and the Women's Indian Association in 1917 by Annie Besant (1847–1933), an Englishwoman who, like many other Westerners, had rejected the West and made India her home. Her co-founders were Sarojini Naidu (1879–1949) and Margaret Cousins (1878–1954), another Englishwoman.

These three women were primarily responsible for pioneering the women's movement in India. They influenced and inspired large numbers of women and men. Annie Besant was jailed by the British for agitating for self-government, called the Home Rule Movement. While in custody, Annie Besant was elected by members to preside over the 1917 session of the INC, the first woman to hold that highly prized office.

Women's associations Sarojini Naidu, with Margaret Cousins, set up the Women's Indian Association (WIA). This later became the nucleus of the All-India Women's Conference (AIWC). Sarojini and Margaret established over 40 branches of the WIA all over India. By 1921, the WIA had 2,700 members,

One of its members was Dr. Muthulakshmi Reddi (1886–1968), a close colleague of Margaret Cousins and the first woman medical graduate in Madras. She gave up her large practice to work for women's emancipation, then went further, in 1927, by becoming the first Indian woman legislator when nominated to the Legislative Council of Madras. She was subsequently elected deputy speaker of the council but resigned in 1930 to protest the arrest of Mahatma Gandhi by the British.

The National Council of Women was formed in 1925. It was established to coordinate the work of various women's organizations in the country. This led to the establishment of the AIWC in 1926.

> "You have done something that may serve to redeem for one moment the shame and degradation of your fallen manhood. In giving to a mere woman, the woman who for years and years rocked the cradle and sang lullabies, that national standard which is the emblem of your own regeneration, you have gone back to the earliest inspiration that built your civilization and admitted the woman a co-sharer and a comrade in the secular and spiritual evolution of a people."
>
> *Sarojini Naidu*
> *addressing a meeting of the INC*
> *on being elected its president in 1925*

The AIWC started off with 47 women from different parts of the country. Their top priority was the promotion of education for girls and the drawing up of a memorandum on educational reform to present to an All-Parties' Conference. While working on the memorandum, the delegates realized that abolishing child marriage was a necessary first step toward getting girls educated. A delegation was sent to press for the enactment of the Child Marriage Restraint Bill, which had been introduced at the All-Parties' Conference. The bill was passed in 1929 which made it illegal to marry a boy under 18 or a girl under 15. This was later amended to 21 and 18 respectively.

The AIWC members believed that it was very important to mobilize political support. The constitution of the AIWC was thus amended in 1938 to permit political activity. By this time, the AIWC had grown into a powerful body of women activists, reformers, and educationists.

> "I am uncompromising in the matter of woman's rights. In my opinion, she should suffer no legal disability not suffered by man. I should treat the daughters and sons on a footing of perfect equality."
>
> *Mahatma Gandhi*

> "For my part I am partial to the women of India, and the more I have wandered around this great country, the more I have felt a certain pride in our womenfolk."
>
> *Jawaharlal Nehru*

Women militants

Chafing over the slow progress of the independence movement and rejecting petitionary politics as insufficient, many Indian nationalists, including women, took to the streets in an open display of violence in order to hasten the British out of India.

Bhikhaji Rustom Cama (1861–1936) was a member of an affluent Parsi family from Bombay. She was one of the earliest Indian revolutionaries. Based in London from 1902, she sent revolutionary literature and arms to India from Paris. Then at the Socialist Congress in Stuttgart, Germany, in August 1907, she unfurled a flag she had designed, signifying freedom for India.

Santi Das, along with her colleague Suniti, shot dead a notorious district magistrate of Comilla, in West Bengal, in December 1931. Both were sentenced to life in prison.

Bina Das tried to assassinate the governor of Bengal in 1932 and was sentenced to seven years' imprisonment.

Among those who took part in a raid on the Chittagong Armory in 1933 was Kalpana Dutt, who was sentenced to life imprisonment.

It was Mohandas Karamchand Gandhi (1869–1949) who showed people that there was a third way of fighting for freedom, a way much different from petitionary politics and revolutionary violence. He encouraged *satyagraha* ("SEHT-yah-grah-hah")—non-violent

disobedience. (Literally, *satyagraha* means holding fast to the truth.) This proved to be Gandhi's greatest contribution, not just to India, but to the world. He helped people to realize that they should resist wrong, even if the resistance meant enduring physical assault, imprisonment, or death.

Since independence

India received its independence on August 15, 1947. There was great joy that British domination had finally ended, even though the country had been divided. The government leaders then were farsighted visionaries. Honesty, loyalty, and commitment to the people were their guiding principles.

The Indian Constitution gives women and children inviolable rights on par with men. The Ministry of Women and Child Development tackles the specific problems of women and children, while the National Commission on Women champions women's issues. Indira Gandhi (1917–1984), the country's first woman prime minister, was particularly sensitive to women's issues.

Women's and children's literacy is addressed nationally by nongovernmental organizations. Women, including the Muslim women in *purdah*, are becoming more vocal about their grievances. Women of all classes are working outside their homes.

Girls at a chemistry lesson in school.

chapter three

Women in Society

W hen India became independent in 1947, the male-female ratio was 1,000-987. Today, almost 50 years later, it is down to 1,000-927, perhaps the lowest in the world. Behind the statistics are years of discrimination against women.

Many factors combine to make life tough for women, particularly rural women. Infant mortality in India is among the highest in the world—96 out of 1,000 births. Because children (especially sons) are considered a family's wealth, the result is that women face many more pregnancies, which take their toll over the years. The rate is aggravated by the fact that pregnant and nursing women are terribly undernourished. Maternal mortality is also high—34 out of 10,000. Only 33% of pregnant women have access to professional medical help when their babies are born. That is because India spends less than 1% of its gross national product on public health.

However, as the country has modernized, the benefits have trickled down to affect the lives of women. The vast road and rail network in India helps people, including women and children, to migrate to other states in search of work.

In urban areas, particularly among the middle class, access to education, advanced technology, and freedom of thought and expression have transformed women's lives. Women go to school and college and work before marriage. In fact, the better-educated woman can pay less dowry (the sum paid to the groom before marriage). Men who advertise for brides in newspapers often include "Working woman preferred" as an added criterion.

Opposite: Women protesting in front of the Supreme Court.

Right: A woman selling vegetables in an open-air market.

Indian women have made their mark in virtually every field. Women fly commercial planes, belong to leading scientific bodies, and are excellent entrepreneurs, industrialists, doctors, and engineers. Since 1992, women have also held commissioned ranks in the defense services.

The influence of religion

Hindu scriptures say that for a man to attain salvation, a son must perform the last rites. Men fear that if they have no son, their soul will find no peace. Naturally, people want to ensure that they have at least one surviving son. Discrimination thus starts even before birth.

Despite this, religious women like Mirabai (c. 1504–c. 1550) and Sharada Devi (1853–1920) attracted vast numbers of followers.

Sharada Devi Born in Bankura, West Bengal, in 1853, Sharada Devi was married to Gadadhara, the mystic who came to be known as Ramakrishna Paramahansa, when she was 6 years old. Ramakrishna was an extraordinary person. He had no formal education, yet his wisdom was the envy of many learned people of his time.

Married to such a man at such an early age, it was inevitable that Sharada Devi would absorb spirituality from her mystic husband. She too practiced severe austerities to attain salvation. Ramakrishna died in 1886 when Sharada Devi was just 33. She then took on his mantle and preached the gospel of universal love. Sharada Devi died in 1920. Sharada Math, an institution set up by her followers, runs hospitals and schools and works extensively in rural areas.

What is amazing about Sharada Devi is that, unlike most women married to great people, she chose to do something in her own right even though her first priority was her husband. For a woman at that time, it was revolutionary thinking.

How many children ...?

In a small rural town, you may see three boys and two girls playing in front of a house. If you ask the man standing there how many children he has, he will say, "I have three children."

When you say, "But I count three boys and two girls. Aren't the girls yours?" the man will reply, "Oh, but they are girls. They will belong to someone else's family the moment they are married."

The Christian missionaries

The apostle Thomas came to India to preach Christianity in A.D. 52 and is reported to have established a small church in the Mylapore district of the southern city of Madras. Since then, Christianity has grown into one of the major religions in India, through the efforts of Christian missionaries from all over the world. They built many schools, colleges, and hospitals.

After India became independent in 1947, there was a general hue and cry raised against many Christian missionaries because most people had the impression they were in the country to do nothing but to convert people.

One of the few missionary operations that had universal approval is the Missionaries of Charity in Calcutta founded by Mother Teresa, an Albanian-born Roman Catholic nun, who has been awarded a Nobel Peace Prize for her work. Nuns from the Missionaries of Charity pick up the destitute and the dying from the streets and minister to them. They also run orphanages. Today, the Missionaries of Charity do their important work in missions all over the world.

Mother Teresa has spent a lifetime in India helping the poor.

sculpture of a dancing girl was unearthed. Dance, music, painting, and sculpture are integral parts of Indian life.

Culture is a living, everyday affair in the lives of the majority of Indians. From clothes to adornment and ritual, everything is essentially Indian.

The *sari* ("SAH-ree") is the most common women's dress. Consisting of a 6-yard length of cloth wrapped gracefully round the body, it is worn in different styles in different parts of India. The majority wear it with the free end draped over the left shoulder.

Less restricting than the *sari*, the *salwar kameez* ("SEHL-wahr kheh-MEEZ"), a dress of northern Punjab, is fast becoming popular all over India. It is a two-piece outfit with long, loose, gathered trousers and a knee-length top. A loose, 6.5-foot length of cloth called a *dupatta* ("doo-PEHT-tah") is gracefully draped across the shoulders.

Few women wear Western-style dresses.

Dance

For many centuries, only men were allowed to perform in public. Women, especially those who belonged to higher castes, were forbidden to dance. Women dancers were regarded as prostitutes and "cheap," even in the late 1940s, both in North and South India. In the North only *nautch* ("notch") girls—girls who performed in public for the pleasure of men—sang and danced.

The *sari*, the national costume of Indian women, is made up of yards of material gracefully draped round the body.

A vibrant culture

Indians are proud of their ancient past. Archeological evidence points to a flourishing civilization by the banks of the river Indus as far back as 3500 B.C. The earliest evidence of formalized dance in the region was found in Mohenjo-Daro (2500 B.C.), where a

Classical dance In the South, the *devadasi* ("they-vah-dah-see") system kept music and dance alive. *Devadasis* were originally young women who sang and danced only in temples to please the gods. These women were not only gifted in the arts but were also highly educated. In time, however, the *devadasis* were exploited by wealthy male patrons, and the system is now banned by law.

Today, however, dance and music enjoy vast popularity throughout India. There are several schools where these fine arts are taught, and both women and men dancers and musicians travel the world giving public performances.

That such a thing has happened is mainly the work of one woman, Rukmini Devi Arundale (1914–86). In 1936, she established Kalakshetra, the first dance school in Madras. Since then, dance schools have become very popular. Other famous dance schools are the Bharatiya Kala Kendra in New Delhi and Darpana in Ahmedabad. A new dance school, the Nritya Gram, is run by Protima Bedi on the lines of the ancient Indian schools which believed in harmonizing with nature.

Noteworthy dancers include Yamini Krishnamurti and Balasaraswati, who was a *devadasi*. She had no rival when it came to *abhinaya* ("a-bhee-nah-yah"), the art of expression without words, similar to mime.

Indrani Rehman revived the lost art of the graceful Odissi dance. This form of dance, which originated in the eastern state of Orissa, had nearly died out when Indrani decided to study and perform it. Sanjukta Panigrahi and Sonal Mansingh, the daughter of a for-mer governor of the state of Gujarat, brought Odissi to the homes of the people. Both these women dedicated their lives to the study and popu-larization of Odissi dance, in order to ensure its continuation. In this, they were supported by their families.

Raja and Radha Reddy, a husband and wife team, are the best-known Kuchipudi dancers in the country. Kuchipudi is the native dance of the southern state of Andhra Pradesh, which

Balasaraswati was a virtuoso in the art of *abhinaya.*

Raja and Radha Reddy revived and popularized.

Today thousands of Indian girls and young women are studying the different schools of classical dance in institutions of dance and music.

A tribal folk dance.

Modern dance When the modern dance troupe founded by Ananda and Tanushree Shankar, a husband and wife team, gave their first performance, people loved the colorful costumes, the catchy music, and the whole spectacle of choreographed light and sound. Ananda and Tanushree adapt classical and folk dance styles and movements and incorporate them into the dances they perform. MamataShankar, Anand's sister, also runs a dance troupe.

Folk dances Folk dances are found across the length and breadth of the country, but the best-known ones are the tribal dances of Bastar in Madhya Pradesh and the Santhals of West Bengal. Men and women dance and sing together in long, swaying rows, arms intertwined behind them. The atmosphere is infectious as the accompanying instruments throb with the beat of the rhythm.

Music

Indians love music. At any picnic, even on the bus, the one overwhelming noise comes from the radio blaring popular movie songs. Movies often become box office hits simply because of the songs.

The acknowledged queen of movie songs is Lata Mangeshkar, who has enthralled young and old for more than four decades. There was a time when no movie was considered complete without one of Lata's songs in it. Today there are many playback singers whose songs are featured in popular movies, but Lata is still the favorite. Lata is internationally known as she has performed all over the world.

Classical music The two styles of classical music are the South Indian, called Carnatic, and the North Indian, called Hindustani. Much of classical music is devotional. Public performances of classical music, like classical dance, used to be given only by men. Then in the early 1900s, women like Kesaribai

Kerkar and Begum Akhtar defied public opinion and sang on stage. It is remarkable that their parents allowed them to be taught by male *gurus* ("goo-roos"), or teachers, at a time when young women were neither seen nor heard!

M.S. Subbulakshmi's devotional music draws huge crowds at concerts. She has acted in devotional movies and has been honored with many awards. Classical vocalist Kishori Amonkar is also very popular.

Today, classical music, both vocal and instrumental, is taught in music schools. Music has become unisex, with women playing the *tabla* ("tub-lah"), or Indian drums, traditionally played only by men. Twenty-something Anuradha Pal is the youngest professional woman tabla player in India today.

Pop music A tiny percentage of the population listens to pop music. Yet even popular movie songs borrow from Western pop music! Usha Uthup was the first person to make a name for herself singing pop songs in the late 1950s. Her music is an irresistible mix of Western and Indian. Among those following in her tradition are Jasmine Bharucha (who has been featured on MTV), Penny Vaz, and Alisha Chinai.

The art scene

Paris-trained Amrita Shergill was the first modern Indian painter to make an impression on the international art world.

Athough only in her 20s when she died, she left a rich legacy for art aficionados.

The modern art scene has seen the rise of many artists. The works of Anjolie Ela Menon (b. 1940) are greatly sought after. A natural painter since her schooldays, Anjolie studied art formally in Moscow. Her paintings have a luminous quality that reminds one of

Anjolie Ela Menon is one of the best-known modern artists in India.

Russian icons. Anjolie's work, like that of many Indian artists, is displayed in major galleries all over the world.

The reach of education

The Indian Constitution guarantees free elementary education, yet many children do not go to school. This is partly because parents, especially in rural areas and urban slums, need their children to earn money, and partly because the quality of education is so uninspiring that students prefer to avoid school.

In the late 19th century, at a time when women were denied education, three enterprising women, Pandita Ramabai, Anandibai Joshee, and Kadambini Ganguly studied in universities abroad. Yet India today has a lower literacy rate than any other country. The majority of schools are run by the government, and like most enterprises run by the state, these educational institutions are poorly equipped, badly managed, and understaffed.

In rural areas, children cannot be spared from work for the luxury of school. Gorabai, who lives in a remote desert village in Rajasthan, has four children. Her husband is a potter. None of their children go to school because every hand counts.

Realizing the problems the poor have in sending working children to school,

An English class at a women's university.

nongovernmental organizations now run literacy classes in rural areas that suit the working pattern of the villages. If it is harvest time, schools close so that everyone can help in the fields. In cities, schools close for the summer, but in villages schools remain open because it is a relatively free time.

The national literacy level today is 52.11% (men 63.86%, women 39.42%). The government has finally realized the value of educating girls. Girls are given free uniforms and an annual grant of $60 as an incentive to attend school. Maharashtra has implemented a successful program to find sponsors for a girl's education so that the financial burden for her family is eased.

Creative writers

Nearly 3,000 years ago, Vac, the daughter of the sage Ambhirna in Vedic times, wrote, "I am the queen, the gatherer-up of treasures/Most thoughtful, first of those who merit worship."

Vac was the first of a long line of devotees whose writings form a part of the ancient Vedas and Puranas. Ironically, women of later generations were forbidden to read these sacred books.

As discrimination increased, women were kept away from books. Yet their desire to learn never died.

Early in the 20th century, Swarna Kumari Debi, elder sister of the great Indian novelist and poet, Rabindranath Tagore, became Bengal's first-published

"Can a person who buys a place in a marketplace be disturbed by noise? Or alarmed by the roar of the surf if he builds a house by the sea? Can we let praise or blame of the world perturb us when we are born into the world?"
Akka Devi, 12th-century woman writer

Women writers

Only recently have women writers begun expressing their emotions freely and without reference to religion.

Jamuneswari Khataniyar, an Assamese poet who died before she was 24, wrote a touching verse on the subject of women's enduring silence over their deepest personal concerns.

In silence my hopes rise and sink,
In silence I find my heart's delight,
In silence I walk through eternal night,
In silence I bear my defeat and
  triumph,
In silence I die, in silence am born.

woman novelist. One of her themes was the freedom struggle, which was uppermost in people's minds. Women were equally fired by the movement for independence. They became ardent educationists, journalists, and writers.

Asia's first feminist publishing house

Kali For Women is a publishing house started by Urvashi Butalia (above left) and Ritu Menon (above right) in 1984 for writing on and by women. It is the first publishing house for feminist literature in South Asia and was set up as a non-profitable trust. This means that profits from the organization are ploughed back into the trust. It gives them a chance to publish the kind of women-related material that no one else publishes.

Almost 99% of the writers published by Kali are women. It is not that they are averse to men, but, according to Urvashi, "Very few men are interested in writing about women." Kali was born because of the need to make women's issues the central concern. It was also because there was no significant writing on women by Indians. Those who were writing on Indian women's issues were mostly Westerners who came with huge grants and produced scholarly material with Western perceptions. Urvashi and Ritu wanted to prove that Indians could produce relevant, quality books too.

Kali For Women produces three types of books: academic books for scholars; popular writing like novels and short stories written in regional languages; and pamphlets and small books meant for activists working at the grassroots level.

The pamphlets and small books are what Ritu and Urvashi value most. They feel their pamphlets reach nongovernmental organizations and others who desperately need their information. Kali has given women writers a step up that was badly needed.

Bengal was the first state to educate women beginning in 1849. Therefore, the contributions of Bengali women to literature have been substantial.

Toru Dutt (1856–1877) was born into a Christian Bengali family. When she was 13, she went to England with her parents and lived and studied there for four years. She also studied in France, and in 1876 published a collection of poems, *A Sheaf Gleaned from French Fields*, and later, *Ancient Ballads and Legends of Hindusthan*. She also wrote a novel in French.

The independence movement produced some of the best protest literature by women. Indian writers like Ismat Chugtai, Qurratulain Haider, Amrita Pritam, Mahadevi Verma, and Ashapurna Devi, to name a few, have had their works translated into several languages. Some of their novels have been adapted for television and movies.

Sarojini Naidu was India's first woman governor, but she was also a well-known poet. Her poems are among the texts included in school curricula. Among her better-known works is a collection of poems called *The Sceptered Flute*.

Scores of women are writing in several Indian languages, as well as in English. Today they write freely and openly about their lot in life and other personal and emotional issues that were considered taboo even as recently as 20 years ago.

Anita Desai

Anita Desai's first novel, *Cry the Peacock*, made people sit up and take notice. Many other novels followed, winning her world acclaim. Anita, born in 1937, is currently a professor at the Massachusetts Institute of Technology in the United States when she is not writing. Her stories give the reader an insight into India.

One of her shorter novels, *Village by the Sea*, portrays the joys and sorrows of a poor Indian family. In fact, its subtitle is "An Indian Family Story." It is the story of a sister and brother, Lila and Hari. Lila is 13 and Hari only 12, yet as the eldest children of a poor family that has fallen on hard times, the responsibility of the entire family rests on their young shoulders. With an ailing mother and a drunken father, Lila and Hari desperately try to keep poverty at bay, with little success. Then Hari goes away to Bombay in search of a job.

Things begin to change. Lila has to cope with the burden of running the house without Hari. Hari comes back from Bombay with positive plans for the future.

What makes *The Village by the Sea* so moving is the simplicity of the narrative and the superb craftsmanship of Anita Desai's writing. Lila and Hari's story could well be the story of thousands of ordinary families.

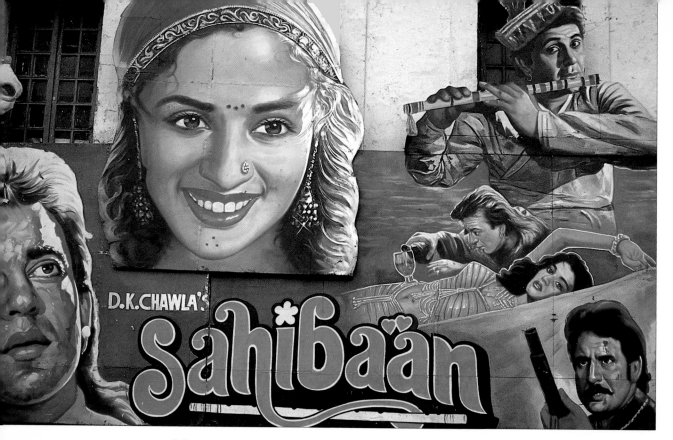

A movie poster featuring Madhuri Dixit, a well-known actress.

Movie mania

Indians are crazy about movies. Few know that the Indian movie industry is the world's largest or that India was the first Asian country to screen movies.

Modern Indian movies are full of violence and sexual innuendo. There are suggestive dances and lewd scenes—but a kiss? Unlikely! Social scientists say part of the violence against women in India is because of the way women are portrayed in movies.

Lead actresses command high salaries, but never as much as lead actors. Most movie stars work in commercial cinema, with its dose of violence, sex, and predictable situations. Some stars, however, are known best for their performances in fine art movies. These do not draw as large crowds as popular movies, but it is these movies that win international acclaim and awards. The late Smita Patil, Shabana Azmi, and, recently, Dimple Kapadia have all turned in superb performances.

Themes in fine art movies often concern women's problems like loneliness, a busy husband, an involvement with a third person, oppression, and exploitation by higher-caste men.

Aparna Sen is one of the finest directors in the country. Her movies *36, Chowringhee Lane* and *Paroma* reflect the personality of two completely different women. In *36, Chowringhee Lane*, Aparna portrays an old Anglo-Indian schoolteacher who stayed on in India when many like her left for Britain during the independence movement. She and her brother live on memories of a bygone era whose glory will never return. It is a poignant movie, a tribute to both the director and the lead actress, Jennifer Kendall Kapoor.

Paroma is the story of a typical Indian woman—some man's daughter, a mother, or a grandmother, never a person in her own right. Into her world steps a young photographer who is enchanted with her. A relationship slowly develops. Initially Paroma is horrified at her reactions and responses, but slowly realizes that she deserves to be appreciated for herself.

An interesting fact about the Indian movie industry is that the stars of Hindi movies often come from the southern states. Hema Malini and Sridevi, both top stars, are from Tamil Nadu where they speak Tamil. Waheeda Rehman is from Andhra Pradesh where they speak Telugu. Very few North Indian movie stars are popular in South India.

Women directors have also grown in number. Mira Nair's *Salaam Bombay*, a moving story about street children, won an award at the Cannes Film Festival. Her movie *Mississippi Masala* deals with the problems of Indian immigrants in the United States. Oscar-winning actor Denzel Washington played the male lead.

Sai Paranjpye directs movies that deal with contemporary problems but are devoid of the usual mix of violence and sex. Full of humor, irony, and pathos, her movies are almost always popular.

Industry and Business

In 1950, there were 280,947 women working in factories, which constituted 11.33% of the total labor force of 2,479,379. In addition, there were women working on plantations, in mines, in agriculture, and in the domestic sector. Today, 26,800,000 women work in the private and public sectors alone. Though the number has gone up substantially, it is only 14% of the total workforce.

What has changed dramatically is the number of middle-class women who now work. Also, women are now working everywhere—in offices, in laboratories, hospitals, and airlines. In fact, it would be difficult to think of a profession where there are no women!

Becoming an entrepreneur is difficult for an Indian woman. She starts out with many constraints men do not face. She has to run her home, look after her husband and children, and keep her in-laws pleased, if she happens to be living with them, in addition to her work. She cannot keep late hours. Business entertainment that may include males is frowned upon. So a businesswoman has many hurdles to cross even before she starts her venture.

Hundreds of success stories are told of ordinary women who started out with virtually nothing, yet have large business empires today. Sumati Morarjee ran a

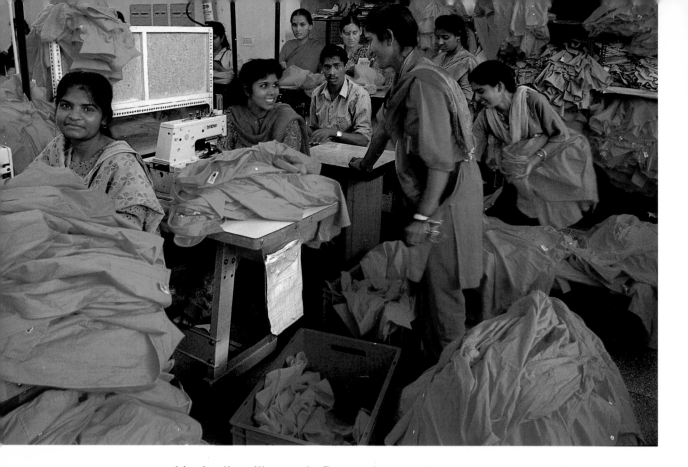

Many rural women who come to the city to find work are hired in garment factories.

shipping line till recently. Parameshwar Godrej looks after a part of the business interests of the vast Godrej empire. Ritu Nanda launched slick-looking cooking ranges called Nicky Tasha. Shahnaz Hussain's herbal cosmetics have an international market.

Many women entrepreneurs are in the garment business. Most of them start with very little capital. In the beginning, they work out of home, employing a master cutter, a tailor, and perhaps one errand boy. The demand for trendy, ready-made garments is so great that, within five years, they have a flourishing business. Nalini Sharma, one such entrepreneur, runs a company called Nalini's. She now has showrooms

all over the country and some abroad.

Another familiar tag, Ritu's, comes with Ritu Kumar's designs. Ritu revived the near-forgotten art of *zardozi* ("zahr-doh-see")—embroidery with gold thread. She now provides employment to hundreds of women, all making *zardozi* outfits. Prices for her outfits range from $300 to nearly $3,000, depending on the weight of gold thread used.

But the garment industry aside, can Indian women succeed in male-dominated fields? The most recent success story belongs to an ordinary housewife who now runs a vast business empire. Starting with leather exports, Rita Singh branched out into mines, metals, and other allied products. Next on her agenda is starting an airline! Her business empire is called Mesco. There is an entire industrial area on the outskirts of Delhi called the Mesco Industrial Area.

The cooperative movement has also led to successful business ventures for women. The Lijjat Papad enterprise is by women for women. It is remarkable not just for its phenomenal growth but also for the way it has brought together people of different communities. It was started by housewives in Bombay and Pune to provide employment to those women who could not leave their homes in search of work, yet desperately needed to supplement the family income. The *papad* ("peh-pehd") is a thin, flat, round disc made of ingredients like rice and lentils. Women make the *papad* at home and deliver them to the cooperative office, where they are paid instantly. The organization markets them under the brand name Lijjat Papad.

The Lijjat network employs thousands of women today. So successful have they been that they have now diversified into other products, including detergents.

Journalism

As late as the 1970s, a woman who worked at a newspaper only covered social or cultural events. She was never allowed to cover hard news or to write editorial commentary. Today, however,

"There are more women journalists now than there were even 10 years ago. But even today, the thrust is political, so important subjects like development are considered 'soft.' Editors only look at sensational stories. Yet a quiet revolution is taking place all over the country. A responsible journalist must report what is happening, both good and bad."

Usha Rai

women are everywhere—in the print media, video magazines, radio, and television, and commenting on all subjects.

Usha Rai Usha Rai (b. 1940) started her career with the *Indian Express*, put in over 20 years with the *Times of India*, and is now back with the *Indian Express* as development editor. Her assignments have taken her all over the world—to

Usha Rai, an outspoken journalist and feminist.

The work of the first woman cartoonist in India, Manjula Padmanabhan, has appeared in all the major daily newspapers across the country.

the Amazon, Australia, Europe, and the United States. On the environment, education, or women's issues, Usha Rai's comments are taken seriously.

Amita Malik An equally formidable woman is Amita Malik, a veteran broadcaster and critic known for her bold, fearless interviews and her astute, acerbic writing. Her radio interviews have been broadcast over foreign networks. In 1993, she was awarded the prestigious Ramnath Goenkla Prize for her long and eventful years in journalism.

Entering the fray Women journalists and broadcasters are no longer kept away from political commentary. Tavleen Singh, a brisk, no-nonsense writer with a gift for gut issues, is eagerly read. Kalpana Sharma is a crusader for justice for women and children.

Nalini Singh, who makes daringly different programs for television, takes the camera to areas the government fears to tread. Total impartiality is the hallmark of Nalini's programs. One featured a graphic description of booth-capturing during elections, where corrupt politicians send thugs to take over polling booths, throw out the legitimate voters, and stuff the ballot boxes. It was filmed at great personal risk.

Women were earlier not sent to areas where terrorism or violence were common. They are everywhere today—in Kashmir, in Punjab at the height of the terrorist problem with separatists, and in Ayodhya in the midst of the free-for-all when the Babri mosque was razed to the ground in December 1992 by Hindus who claimed it had been built over the birthplace of the God Rama.

Manjula Padmanabhan The country's first woman cartoonist, Manjula began her career with a weekly cartoon strip called "Double Talk" for *The Sunday Observer* in Bombay. Her daily strip,

"Suki," appears now in the *Pioneer*. She is also an illustrator of repute. Her work has appeared in all major dailies and magazines. She illustrates profusely for children, who love her magical fantasy.

Manjula is also a playwright and short-story writer. Her writing reflects her concern with women's issues without being stridently feminist. Her play *Lights Out* deals with the problem of rape and people's reaction to it. "People," she says, "feel that a problem will go away if they simply don't look at it. So mostly they ignore even the most glaring atrocities if it doesn't touch their lives. I want to show people that rape can come into their sitting room." The play was staged in Bombay and Delhi. *The Mating Game* is a hard-hitting commentary on the evil dowry system. The point she makes is that the vile practice will remain as long as the women themselves become party to it.

Broadcast media Satellite television and video have become a popular alternative to movies. The government-owned television network, Doordarshan, reaches millions of people, but the fare offered is insipid and unattractive. It is also the medium for government propaganda. Doordarshan, which had a monopoly on news reporting until recently, now has competition from video programs like Newstrack.

Newstrack is the first video unit to bring hard news to people. Run by a gutsy woman, Madhu Trehan, Newstrack airs interviews with terrorists and clips of momentous occasions taken at great risk to its correspondents. Once during the elections, Newstrack captured on film a person being beaten to death. Its coverage of the Mandal riots (riots sparked by the government's policy of reserving seats in government jobs and institutions on the basis of caste) brought praise. Though viewership has fallen in the last year, if there is a good, in-depth story on Newstrack, people prefer to watch that rather than the government station.

Government

India was one of the first countries to elect a woman prime minister. As far back as 1885, the Indian National Congress had been open to women who spoke, voted, and served as delegates at the annual general meeting of the organization.

In the first election in 1952, 51 women ran and 23 were elected to Parliament, making up 4.4% of the

"... Women must have votes and an equal legal status. But the problem does not end there. It only commences at the point where women begin to affect the political deliberations of the nation."

Mahatma Gandhi

A different way

Unlike militant feminist actions elsewhere, the battle by Indian women for equal rights has been very low-key. They have been persuasive and persistent, but never violent or aggressive.

In 1917, Mr. Montagu, secretary of state for India, received a letter signed by four members from the senate of the Indian Women's University. They wanted an interview to discuss "the women of India."

On December 18, 1917, 14 women led by Sarojini Naidu met Mr. Montagu and the Viceroy Lord Chelmsford. They asked that when the franchise was drawn up, women should be given the same opportunities for representation as men. Mr. Montagu noted in his diary: "We had an interesting deputation from the women asking for education for girls, more medical colleges etc., etc. ... The deputation (was) led by Mrs. Naidu, the poetess, a very attractive and clever woman but I believe a revolutionary at heart. ... They also asked for women's votes. ... They assured me that the Congress would willingly pass a unanimous request for women's suffrage."

Such a resolution was in fact passed by the Calcutta session of the Congress presided over by Annie Besant. It recorded its opinion that "the same tests be applied to women as to men in regard to franchise and eligibility to all elective bodies concerned with the local government and education."

House. In the 1991 election, 33 women formed 6.4% of the House of 520 members. The largest number of women in Parliament was during Rajiv Gandhi's landslide victory after Indira Gandhi's assassination. In all, 421 women ran and 159 won seats, accounting for 7.9% of the House.

It was not till 1926 that women were given rights on the same terms as men in elections for provincial legislative councils. In April of that year, the government gave women the right to sit on the legislative councils. In 1928, the All-India Women's Conference began to demand equal rights for women in all spheres. Mahatma Gandhi gave the movement his blessing.

Vijaya Lakshmi Pandit (1900–1990) was the first woman to serve as minister in a provincial government. The first woman minister in the federal government was Lakshmi Menon. She held the important portfolio of deputy minister in the Ministry of External Affairs in the early 1950s. The galaxy of women who influenced major political decisions in those days reads like a who's who of the freedom movement. Aruna Asaf Ali, Rajkumari Amrit Kaur, Kamaladevi Chattopadhyay, Sucheta Kripalani, and Renuka Ray were but a few of those who raised their voices for the betterment of women and children.

For many years, the only party with women members was the Congress Party. Now there are several others. Some women have chosen to join the more fundamentalist parties in the country. The outspoken Uma Bharati of the Bharatiya Janata Party is more in the news than most of her male colleagues. Renuka Choudhary is a leading personality of a regional party, the Telugu Desam. Sheila Kaul of the ruling Congress government is the minister for housing and urban development. Najma Heptulla is deputy speaker of the upper house of Parliament.

Whatever their party, women in positions of power are working to improve the lot of other women not as fortunate as they. Everyone knows now that where the hands of women are strengthened, that country is well on the way to prosperity.

On the administrative side, women have made inroads too. C. Muthamma was the first woman in the Foreign Service. There are hundreds of women in all branches of administration including defense and the police. There is even an all-women battalion. Kiran Bedi, the first woman police officer, has established a reputation for efficiency and quality of service. Now in charge of prisons, she has brought dramatic changes into prison life.

The judiciary has several women judges. The first woman to be appointed to the Supreme Court was Meera Sahib Fatima Beevi (b. 1927), in 1989. Fatima Beevi was the second woman in the world to be appointed to the supreme court of a country, after Sandra Day

Kiran Bedi, the country's first woman police officer, has made many reforms in the treatment of convicts in prisons.

O'Connor in the United States. Leila Seth became the first woman chief justice of an Indian high court, in 1991.

Medicine and Nursing

The first women doctors, like Anandibai Joshee and Kadambini Ganguly, graduated in the late 1800s, but not many women studied medicine. The government offered special incentives to get them to enroll, and the number of women doctors has grown enormously since those days, but even so is insufficient for today's needs. According to the 1981 census, there were a total of 51,431 women doctors; 10,591 in rural areas and 40,840 in urban areas. The ratio in 1989 was 4,213 female doctors to 7,000 male doctors. The latest available data shows that 6,873 men and 6,516 women are enrolled in medical school.

Women vets

Dr. Sagari Ramdas (left) and Dr. Nitya Ghotge started ANTHRA (Animal Training, Health, Research Services), an organization of women veterinarians. They are committed to improving the health, productivity, and overall welfare of animals in rural areas, knowing that this will help the welfare of the owners.

Both of them have worked as rural vets through different rural development organizations. Sagari holds a master's degree in animal breeding and genetics from the University of California. Nitya specialized as a veterinary surgeon at Bombay Veterinary College. Both have broad professional experience in rural livestock production problems, ranging from tribal to semi-nomadic shepherding systems. As veterinary consultants to nongovernmental organizations, they have developed educational materials. Sagari also uses alternative medicine, particularly homeopathy, for the prevention and cure of diseases.

The two young doctors are particularly concerned about creating awareness among women in livestock-rearing communities about the vital role they play in animal rearing. Their aim is to equip them with the skills to be effective in livestock-rearing. Because they are women in a male-dominated society, they have been able to build better rapport with rural women who are responsible for animal rearing.

Today there are women doctors in every field. Indira Hinduja, head of Gynecology and Obstetrics at KEM Hospital in Bombay, made history when she used, for the first time in India, *in-vitro* fertilization (the test-tube method) to help childless couples have babies.

Prithika Chary of Madras was the first woman in Asia to qualify both as a neurologist and a neurosurgeon.

When India became independent, there was only one nurse to 43,000 people. Though the number of nurses has increased, there are still not enough to meet demand. Most nurses are from Kerala. They are often lured to Persian Gulf countries with promises of better-paying jobs and better working conditions.

There are women in the veterinary services too. The Association of Women Veterinarians of India is a common forum for women vets to discuss current medical issues as well as professional grievances. The greater number of women vets live in towns and cities and confine themselves to treating pets. The more adventurous live in rural areas and get hands-on experience in treating cattle, horses, and poultry. Their aim is to improve the quality of life for people in the villages.

Social work

Social work today is considered as much a profession as any other paid job. Nongovernmental organizations are staffed by women professionals with social commitment.

A number of these women work at the grassroots level, which means that they are based in villages. These villages do not have amenities like piped water or sanitation. It takes a special kind of drive to be able to stay and work with villagers, and many of the women who do have studied in the best schools and colleges, both in India and abroad.

Women activists

More and more women activists have surfaced, pursuing causes where social injustice prevails.

Medha Patkar Throwing in her lot with that of the tribes who live in and around the Narmada river in Madhya Pradesh, Medha Patkar and the organization she founded, Narmada Bachao Andolan (Save Narmada Agitation), serve not just women but all tribal peoples of the area.

The issue they address is political. Since the neighboring state, Gujarat, is starved of water, the government has decided to build a dam across the Narmada river in Madhya Pradesh to provide drinking water for Gujarat. The dam will submerge millions of acres of forest (even though it is degraded forest land) and will displace tribal peoples who have lived in the area for centuries. Medha contends that the dam is not the right solution to the water problems of Gujarat, particularly as the displaced tribal peoples will neither have a home nor a means of livelihood once the forests go.

Medha may or may not win in the end. But she has raised awareness of people-based environmental concerns. She went on a hunger strike to force the government to suspend work on the

dam and reconsider it. Her agitation has mobilized worldwide support, and people as far away as Germany hold candlelight vigils in support of her cause.

Medha Patkar has made it her life's work to improve the lot of tribal women.

Dr. Vasudha Dhagamwar Heading MARG (Multiple Action Research Group), a voluntary organization that provides legal advice to poor and disadvantaged persons, especially in rural areas, is Dr. Vasudha Dhagamwar (b. 1940). MARG offers support to grassroots groups by providing legal advice on social issues. The organization also undertakes field work on problems that confront disadvantaged groups. The work involves research mainly in three areas: displacement of people due to government projects and their rehabilitation, legal literacy, and the problems of women and children. The documented information is disseminated to those affected and to policy makers. MARG also undertakes consultancy work and runs a legal-aid service.

Dr. Dhagamwar, who holds a postgraduate degree from Oxford University and a doctorate in law from London University, is the founder and executive director of MARG. Between 1974 and 1976 she was based in Akkalkua in the Dhule district of Maharashtra, helping

Bhil tribal peoples in their struggle for land. She has written extensively on legal matters, especially those pertaining to tribal affairs. This multi-talented woman also writes short stories in Marathi. Among her major books are *Law, Power and Justice*; *Women and Divorce*; and *Towards a Uniform Civil Code*. MARG publishes valuable documents and books based on field research.

Sports

It has been a mystery to many why a country with a population of 800 million performs so miserably at international sports meets. And this applies equally to men and women. In mythology, women excelled at games of skill. Shakuntala taught her son archery. Most princesses were taught martial arts. Miniature paintings of medieval times show women playing polo.

In modern times, women were not seriously interested in sports until the early 1900s. When the British came to India they brought with them the concept of club life meant for the entertainment of those who had long hours of leisure. It was this exposure to club life that persuaded mothers to let their daughters take part in games and other physical exercise when progressive schools introduced them as part of the school curriculum.

In the 1930s, Rajkumari Amrit Kaur, who later became India's first minister of health, took up competitive tennis in

P.T. Usha in a track event in the 1980 Olympic Games.

the North. Kshama Row, a Sanskrit scholar, also took up tennis seriously.

The Rajkumari Amrit Kaur Scheme was started in the 1950s to train talented young girls for competitive sports. Some talent was unearthed, but Indian women continue to do poorly in sports.

P.T. Usha In 1980, P.T. Usha (b. 1964) was sent to the Moscow Olympic Games. She became India's youngest Olympian in athletics. She won her first international gold for the 400 meter race at the Asian Track and Field Meet in Kuwait in 1983. At the Seoul (Korea) Asian Games in 1986, Usha won four gold medals and a silver. During her decade-long career, no other Indian woman bettered Usha in the 400-meter race.

Bhuvaneswari Kumari Another woman who has won laurels is Bhuvaneswari Kumari (b. 1960). She plays competitive squash, a sport usually associated with men. No Indian sportsperson has won as many ntional titles in a row as Bhuvaneswari has—17! She is also one of the youngest title holders; she won her first title when she was 15.

From the courts to the mountains In May 1984, Bachendri Pal (b. 1954) climbed Mount Everest, the first Indian and the fifth woman in the world to do so. Since then she has been on many expeditions. Other women, inspired by Bachendri, have also taken up mountaineering. One of them, Santosh Yadav (b. 1964), is the only woman to have climbed Mount Everest twice.

Many women now participate in traditionally "male" sports like mountain climbing and golf.

chapter four

Being Woman

t was Mahatma Gandhi who called women out of the seclusion of their homes to join the movement to liberate the country from British rule. As far back as 1919 he had said, "Probably in this peaceful struggle (the nonviolent movement for independence) woman can outdistance man by many a mile. ... I hope that women all over India will take up the challenge and organize themselves. ... If nonviolence is the law of our being, the future is with women."

Article 15 of the Indian Constitution states that "the State shall not discriminate against any citizen on grounds only of religion, race, caste, sex, place of birth."

The Constitution also requires elementary education for both boys and girls. In cities, most children attend some sort of school. In rural areas, women who attend literacy classes to learn to read and write are also being taught to speak up for themselves. This kind of awakening has led to revolutionary happenings.

Opposite: A young rural girl looking out of a window in the abandoned fort where her family has made a home.

Right: This statue depicts Mahatma Gandhi's call to women to fight for India's independence side by side with the men.

Minority women

The majority of people in India are Hindu. The rest are designated as minorities. Even among the Hindus, there are minorities who belong to certain castes and tribes. In the Constitution they are called scheduled castes and tribes and are entitled to special treatment such as reserved places in institutions and jobs.

The religious minorities are governed by religious laws ruling social relationships. These laws are discriminatory to women. Yet, if women choose to go to an Indian court, justice is not denied to them. The court will consider them as petitioners, not as women of any minority. But many women prefer to be bound by archaic customs as the trauma of going to court is too great.

A woman from the small Shiite Muslim sect—the Dawoodi Bohras—on her prayer mat.

They do not know whom to approach, how to file an application, or how to hire a lawyer.

Muslim women Muslims are the largest religious community after Hindus. Indian Muslims follow certain practices that are non-Islamic, for example, discouraging widows from remarrying. These practices restrict women's freedom. Muslim law in India has many provisions that discriminate against the Indian Muslim woman. Her rights of marriage and divorce are not only inferior to those of men but at odds with the demands of modern India.

In Islam, a man may have as many as four wives and the wife has simply to accept it. The majority of Muslim men today may have only one wife, but the provision of four wives exists in law, with the proviso that each wife be treated exactly the same, materially, physically, and emotionally. But in India, this proviso is often ignored, and one or more wives may be abused while the others are feasted. A Muslim woman may not divorce her husband on the grounds of polygamy. Neither can she have more than one husband at a time.

According to Islamic law, a man can divorce his wife at any time by simply uttering three times the word *talaq* ("tah-LAHK"), meaning "I divorce you." He can do so anywhere and at any time, in a fit of anger or as a coldly calculated act. A woman cannot divorce

> "Polygamy is a luxury of the rich and a liability thoughtlessly incurred even by the men of poorer means. ... The harem was the perpetual source of anxiety both for the rich and the poor."
>
> *Mohammad Yasin, Muslim historian*

her husband in this simple manner. Should she want a divorce, she has to go to court—a cumbersome procedure compared to the facility extended to Muslim men.

A man who divorces his wife is not required to provide any maintenance beyond the period of *iddat* ("ID-deht"), or three menstrual cycles, which works out to approximately three months. During *iddat*, the woman is not supposed to have any contact with males who are not close relatives. This restriction on a woman's freedom is rationalized by the argument that if she turns out to be pregnant, there will be no doubt that it is her husband's (or ex-husband's) child. A man who does not want to pay *iddat* maintenance may simply ill-treat the woman and marry another, since he can have more than one wife.

Muslim law makes provision for a woman to be paid *mehar* ("may-her"), a sum agreed upon at the time of marriage. This is to be her sole property. Her husband has no right to it, under Islamic law. In India, however, the *mehar* is often given to the woman's in-laws, and getting it from them is nearly impossible. Another practice that some Indian Muslim husbands resort to is not to consummate the marriage until their wife gives up her right to *mehar*. Many new brides, out of sheer embarrassment (because they live in a joint family and everyone gets to know about it), succumb to this pressure.

A woman courageous enough to take recourse to law and divorce her husband forfeits her right to *iddat* maintenance and *mehar*.

Winds of change are touching the Indian Muslim community too. Women who for years accepted every injustice are beginning to question traditions and practices that discriminate against them. In June 1993, three young *burqah*-clad women from the walled city of Old Delhi, which is a predominantly Muslim area, held a press conference to make public their unhappiness. All three women had been divorced by husbands uttering *talaq* three times. No causes

> "If you have only one wife, walk confidently into your house after a period of absence. If two, stop at the door and listen hard to the sounds of noise inside. For more than two, better go first to the neighbor's house to check that nothing untoward has happened during your absence."
>
> *A Muslim saying*

The Shah Bano case

Shah Bano, a 75-year-old destitute from Indore, Madhya Pradesh, was the first wife of Mohammad Ahmad Khan. She was also his first cousin. His second wife was also his first cousin. Shah Bano had three sons and two daughters. Halima Begum, the second wife, had one son and six daughters.

After 43 years of marriage, Mohammad Khan divorced Shah Bano and threw her out in 1975. He paid her maintenance for two years at $20 per month, after which it was stopped. In April 1978, Shah Bano filed a case before the judicial magistrate of Indore claiming that since Mohammad Khan was a lawyer with an annual income of more than $6,000, she should be paid a maintenance of $50 a month.

In November 1978, Mohammad Khan deposited $300 in payment of her *mehar*. He then claimed he had no further responsibility toward her maintenance.

The court dismissed his plea and asked him to pay her $1 per month. Shah Bano appealed to the High Court, which raised the rate of maintenance to nearly $18 per month. Mohammad Khan then approached the Supreme Court, claiming that under Muslim personal law he had no responsibility for Shah Bano's maintenance. He stated further that the provisions of the Criminal Procedure Code that provided maintenance for a "wife" were not applicable to him. The Supreme Court, after much deliberation, upheld the High Court judgment.

The judgment angered Muslim fundamentalists who claimed that Muslim women were best off under the tenets of the strict Shariah (Islamic) law. It soon became a political issue. Rajiv Gandhi, who was prime minister then, was persuaded that a judgment such as the one the Supreme Court had given would make Muslims feel insecure. Orchestrated by a group of Muslim members of parliament, the protest swelled to a furor. The government decided to nullify the judgment in order to placate fundamentalist Muslims. A bill was passed in Parliament soon after, ironically called the Muslim Women's Bill, that took away from Muslim women what few rights they had. A young Muslim minister, Arif Mohammad Khan, resigned in protest.

Shah Bano was brainwashed into believing that she had been anti-Islamic by going to court. On November 11, 1985, she retracted her statements. Most people, including liberal Muslims, feel the Muslim Women's Bill is a shame on secular India.

had been given for the divorces. No maintenance was given either. The future for them was indeed bleak as they had no formal training of any kind that would enable them to get a job. But these women had the courage to speak up and protest, something that would not have happened in the Muslim community even five years earlier.

Meanwhile, Jamait Al-Hadith, the Muslim legal body, issued a *fatwa* ("FEHT-wah"), or ruling, saying that *talaq* is contrary to the true spirit of Islam. Their ruling has given women much-needed support, but the matter has not yet been resolved, as traditionalists are disputing the ruling, claiming that it is the *fatwa* that is contrary to Islam.

The burqah The *burqah* is a long, loose garment, mostly made of black material that drapes a woman from head to foot. A slit near the eyes allows her limited vision. It is worn by women who observe *purdah*, which is the practice of almost complete segregation from men. It is worn whenever the woman leaves the house, and occasionally in the house as well if she has to be in the presence of men who are not close relatives.

The *burqah* also has intangible connotations. It means that a woman must not mix with men, aside from close relatives.

A *burqah* restricts movement. Modern Indian Muslim women do not wear the *burqah*, but it is very much in evidence in poor, crowded areas. Even in the capital, New Delhi, it is quite common to see *burqah*-clad women in predominantly Muslim areas.

Education The majority of Muslims go to religion-based schools called *madrasa* ("MEH-dreh-sah"). The teachers are *mullahs* ("MOOL-lahs"), or religious men, who are well-versed in the Quran, and that is what the students are taught best. There is minimal teaching of other subjects like English, geography, history, or the sciences. The *mullahs* usually have no knowledge of science or technology, which is why almost all students who attend *madrasa* invariably fail the public examinations. In a situation like this, where boys—who are the privileged sex—get little or no education, it is to be expected that girls are neglected.

Upper-class Muslims There are Muslim women who have made a mark on society. They have been to the best schools and colleges and have traveled extensively. Enlightened Muslims educate their daughters as well as their sons. Many Muslim women hold excellent jobs—women like Sayeeda

"Chastity is not a hothouse growth. ... It cannot be protected by the surrounding wall of the *purdah*. It must grow from within ... let us then with one mighty effort tear down the *purdah*."

Gandhi in Young India, *Feb. 3, 1927*

"Whenever I think of women in *purdah*, cut off from the outside world, I invariably think of a prison or a zoo! How can a nation go ahead if half of its population is kept hidden away in a kind of prison?"

Nehru in Glimpses of World History

Imam, who heads Contract, one of the best advertising agencies in the country. These Muslim women are articulate, educated, and proud of their culture.

Women's contribution Some Muslim women beat the system and made enormous contributions in several fields. Raziya Sultan was the country's first empress. She had great administrative qualities and a sense of justice.

Among musicians, Begum Akhtar is a name connoisseurs of music treasure. At a time when most Muslim women were in *purdah*, she studied music under male *gurus* or teachers. In more recent times, Parveen Sulatana has enchanted packed concert halls with her crystal-clear voice.

It is in movies that Muslim women have made the biggest contributions. The talkies began with the singing stars Khurshid and Nurjehan. Madhubala, Meena Kumari, and Nargis were beautiful women and sensitive artists who became legends. Waheeda Rehman, now retired, was one of the finest dramatic actresses of the silver screen. Mumtaz (called Mumu by her fans), gave up her incredibly successful career to marry an Indian multimillionaire from East Africa. Today, the famous Shabana Azmi (her father is Kaifi Azmi, a well-known Urdu poet) acts mostly in movies with a meaningful story. Shabana is committed to social ideals and campaigns actively for the rights of slum dwellers in Bombay.

Burqah-clad Muslim women incongruously flanked by provocative movie posters.

Christian Women

Christians make up 2.5% of the population and are the largest minority after Muslims. Most Christians are recent converts from Hinduism, so it is not unusual for them to observe caste rules.

Although Christians are more liberal than Muslims, their religious laws also discriminate against women. A man can file a case in court if he suspects his wife of adultery. If a woman suspects adultery, she has to add to that something else, say, sodomy, in order to file a case. Property laws are also biased. A girl is entitled to only half of what her brother inherits.

A Christian girl's upbringing focuses on service to the community. Girls attend good schools and colleges and are trained for a profession. In the past, teaching and nursing were popular choices. Some of the greatest social service institutions in India are run by Christians.

The missionaries' role The earliest formal education was by Christian missionaries. In fact, the first girls' school was established in 1819 by the Female Juvenile Society run by Baptists. On May 7, 1849, the Calcutta Female School was established with 21 girls enrolled.

A Catholic woman in church.

The school began to take shape when John Drinkwater Bethune, a legal member in the governor-general's council in 1848, took an interest in it.

Some of the best hospitals in the country are run by Christians, such as the Christian Medical Colleges at Vellore and Ludhiana. And some of the country's finest Christian doctors have served in these colleges.

Kerala has a large percentage of Syrian Christians. This state was the first to achieve 100% literacy. Nursing is a vocation for which many women in Kerala are renowned. About 50% of the nurses in India are Christians.

Notable Christian women Anna Rajam George was the first woman to enter the Indian Administrative Service, in 1950. Margaret Alva is a minister of state for personnel. When she was deputy minister for youth affairs and sports she did an excellent job of discovering young sports talent.

Jyotsna Chatterjee heads the Joint Women's Programme (JWP), a voluntary agency working specifically on issues that affect Christians. As chairwoman of the National Council of Churches of India, she has been looking into the legal aspects of marriage and divorce. She says, "People think that among the Christians, there is no caste. That is not true. In some ways, they are even more rigid than the Hindus."

When looking for a marriage partner for their children, Christian parents look for the same caste. Christians often wear symbols of Hindu marriage like the *taali* ("tah-lee"), the sacred thread a woman wears to show she is married. Some wear vermilion paste in their hair parting as Hindu women do. A dowry is expected in some parts of the country.

Mary Roy vs Christian personal law

Mary Roy, a Syrian Christian from the state of Kerala, was living in her father's house. On her father's death, the property went to her brother. Since he had to give a part of the inheritance to her, he said he would sell the house and give her a small amount out of that. Mary, who really was quite well-off in her own right—she runs a successful school and owns property—decided she would ask for half of the proceeds of the sale of the house. It was not that she needed the money; she wanted to fight the inequality of the system.

Mary filed a case in court against the state of Kerala. Her contention was that she was being discriminated against simply because she was a woman. The court upheld her case and decided that the verdict be applied with retroactive effect to cases tried from as early as 1951. Since that was virtually impossible, some members of the community have appealed the ruling. At the time of writing, the matter had still not been resolved.

Mary Roy is exceptional because she had the courage to take on her community and its archaic personal laws. Others simply swallow their pride and succumb to pressure.

Jyotsna herself is "Brahmin" Christian. Such a person is Brahmin by caste before conversion to Christianity. The JWP is trying to get laws passed that will give women the same rights as men, especially in marriage and divorce.

Tribal women

Perhaps the most disadvantaged of all are the tribal people; and the women's lives are even tougher than those of men. Their life is hard. They live high in the mountains or on the fringes of forests. Modern amenities like schools and hospitals are not available in many tribal areas. When the government needs to acquire land for development—like building dams—the first to be displaced are tribal people. It is only now that some voluntary agencies and activists, like Medha Patkar, have taken up their cause.

In most tribal areas, women not only work in the house but also in the fields. The Nagas are a warlike tribe in the northeast. As most of the men were traditionally involved in warfare, it fell to the women to clear rough mountainous terrain for cultivation. They practiced *jhoom* ("jeh-hoom"), or shifting cultivation. Cutting down trees, removing boulders, and leveling hillsides were women's work. Most of the villages were built on hilltops, so women had to walk down 500–1,000 feet for water and then up again. Women cooked, husked grain,

Tribal women are perhaps the most disadvantaged of all women in India.

The many faces of a tribal woman

Shamrao Hivale recorded from a priest of the Pardhan tribe of Madhya Pradesh their perception of women in their tribe.

From dawn to dusk in a single day, a Pardhan woman appears in various different forms. When she is sighted stepping out of her house early in the morning, with an empty pot on her head, she portends bad luck. Those starting on a journey or going for a betrothal who are unlucky enough to see her must cancel their plans, for in this form her name is *Khaparadhari* ("khah-pah-rah-DHAH-ri"), an evil spirit carrying a broken bit of earthenware.

But once the same woman returns with a pot full of water, she becomes *Mata Kalsahin* ("mah-THAH KEHL-sah-heen"), the best, the most auspicious of goddesses. Those who see her then worship her by throwing a *pice* ("pyse," or coin) into the pot before proceeding hopefully and joyfully on a journey or with other plans.

Upon her return, when she begins to sweep the kitchen, she is the goddess *Bahiri Batoran* ("bah-HEE-ree bah-THO-rahn") who rids the village of cholera. The moment she steps out to sweep the courtyard and the lane in front of her house, she sinks in status to a common sweeper. Fortunately, her duties include work on livestock, and as she enters the cowshed she becomes *Mata Lakshmi* ("mah-THAH LUCK-shmee"), the goddess of wealth and good fortune.

By midday, she is ready to serve the family with food, so she changes into *Mata Anna Kuari* ("mah-THAH ah-NAH koo-AH-ree"), the goddess of grain.

When the sun goes down, she lights the lamps and is *Mata Dia Motin* ("mah-THAH dee-ah MOH-tin"), the goddess who shines like a pearl. Once she has given her children their last meal of the day, she gently fans them to sleep, thus becoming *Mata Chawar Motin* ("mah-THAH chah-wahr MOH-tin"), the goddess who induces sleep.

looked after children, and worked in the fields. When the work was done, they sat at their looms and wove lengths of cloth with colorful designs. It is the same story today except that the men no longer go to war.

Tribal women in the plains also work very hard. They go into the forest to gather firewood, berries, and honey. Then they look after all the work of the household.

Tribal people are pantheistic and live in harmony with nature. They worship the sun, the moon, the stars, the trees, and rivers around them. Because of this, they are traumatized more than others when displaced.

When it comes to freedoms—of expression, marriage, or divorce—the tribal woman is much better off than her counterpart in the so-called organized society. A tribal girl marries in her late teens or early 20s. If the marriage fails, she is free to divorce and marry again. Widowhood is not something to be afraid of as there is no stigma attached to it. The community allows a widow to marry again. Many tribes, like the Garos and the Khasis of the northeast and certain tribes in South India, are matrilineal. It is the women who inherit property and therefore their position is strong and stable.

Verrier Elwin, a social anthropologist who lived for years with tribal people, says that tribal women seldom abuse their freedom. They go to the market, dance and sing in public, and converse freely with men. Even after marriage a tribal woman is allowed to be herself.

All this sounds idyllic. But the harshness of daily living is so grim that few would like to be in their place. When they come into cities to sell their wares, they are often cheated. Rapes of tribal women are common. Unable to fight the system of a city that they know nothing about, most of these women simply do not protest. When they do, the police, who are supposed to protect them, support the offenders instead.

Things are slowly changing in India. As literacy reaches tribal women, they are learning about their rights. They are slowly coming out of the forests to look for jobs in cities. Christian missionaries train young tribal girls to be domestics so that they can earn a decent living.

The working woman

The most important change that has taken place since independence is the phenomenal growth of the middle class. One reason is that more and more women are contributing to the family income. They work either as professionals or are self-employed.

The 1981 census gathered statistics on the number of women employed in different sectors of the economy. Their jobs ranged from doctors and surgeons (including veterinarians) to journalists, artists, and many other professions. Since then the number of working women has more than doubled.

Working women in urban areas, especially those who hold reasonably well-paid jobs, prefer to limit their families to two children. Some prefer not to have any children at all as it takes them away from their work for long periods. Maternity leave is generally three months. Those who are lucky to

A working mother

Anita Jaisinghani is an artist with the children's magazine *Target,* published by Living Media. Anita's son, Aneesh, is now 14. She used her maternity leave and went back to work three months after her son was born. She was able to do that because they lived with her in-laws, and her mother-in-law volunteered to look after the baby. Anita went back to work confident that her son would be well looked after.

Why has she not had another child, she is asked frequently. "I can't afford it," she says. "Bringing up one child is difficult for a working woman. I am grateful to my mother-in-law for helping me with Aneesh. But it would be unfair to ask her to look after one more! Besides, it means taking time off from work. I can ill afford to do that. I'll lose my job!"

Women in selected occupations (most recent available statistics)

	Rural	Urban
Doctors and surgeons (including dental and veterinary surgeons)	10,591	40,840
Veterinarians	107	130
Poets, authors, journalists, and related workers	547	2,194
Sculptors, painters, photographers	6,123	9,152
Composers and performing artists	36,368	16,710
Hotel and restaurant managers, housekeepers, matrons, and stewards (domestic and institutional)	2,338	3,306
Cooks, waiters, bartenders, and related workers (domestic and institutional)	39,221	57,536
Maids and other housekeeping service workers	120,431	352,903
Domestic servants	96,556	308,467

be living with older members of the family leave the infant in their care. That way, they have fewer worries because they know the baby is loved and well cared for.

Organizations that spend vast sums of money in training their employees when they join them are hesitant to hire young women. They feel that these women will be sure to marry and leave their job. Therefore, it would be a waste of money and time to employ women. The other factor is maternity leave.

Three months, employers feel, is a lot of time away from work. Also, once the baby arrives, it is believed that women's efficiency suffers, as their mind is more on the baby.

Domestic workers

Life in India is comparatively easier for the middle and upper classes because domestic help is available. Domestic workers help with housework. They sweep, wash floors, dust, make beds, cook, wash dishes and clothes, clean toilets, and generally do any other work their employers ask them to. In homes with smaller incomes, one domestic worker may do all the work with the wife doing the cooking. In wealthier homes, there may be three workers who handle separate jobs—cook, cleaner, nanny.

In 1981, there were 405,023 women domestic workers in the country. The number of domestic workers has increased in the last decade, but the percentage of men who work at such jobs has gone down because job opportunities for them have increased.

Women domestic workers in Bombay are very well organized. They work in a minimum of four houses. Their day begins at 5 in the morning and by the time they get home to their *chawl*

("chah-awl"), or room in a slum, it is 6 or 7 in the evening. Then they attend to their own household chores. Their children are often neglected and get into bad company unless there is someone older to keep an eye on them.

Domestics are often exploited. They are underpaid and overworked. They have no days off. Raises are virtually

Many women in cities work in offices, but mainly in clerical positions.

Two domestics

Sivamma has been working in the upper-class Cuffe Parade area in Bombay for the last 30 years. She has managed to save enough to buy a small plot of land and build a house in her native state of Karnataka. Her daughter married a skilled worker who has a job in a Persian Gulf country. She could retire quite happily but she cannot think of giving up her work and sitting idle. It's a luxury she is not used to!

Nafisa is a refugee from Bangladesh living in Delhi. She is only 10, but she has been working as a domestic for as long as she can remember. She does all the work that an older person does—washes clothes, chops vegetables, dusts, makes beds, takes the children for walks, washes dishes—but she gets less than half the salary of an adult domestic. She is given leftovers to eat and made to sleep on the floor. She cannot go back to her parents' house because they have too many children to look after. Until she grows up and learns some skills, Nafisa's life is misery.

The major newspapers are chockfull of matrimonial ads. Arranged marriages are still the norm in India.

unheard of. Sometimes women domestics are sexually abused by the master of the house.

Domestic workers have no organized body like a trade union to take up their cause. In Bombay, however, women domestic workers can dictate their terms because the demand for domestics far exceeds the supply. In Bombay, a domestic worker can earn between $100 and $150 a month, working in three to four homes—an excellent salary for a domestic worker.

In well-off homes today, people will pay almost anything for a good female domestic worker. But the domestic worker may soon be a luxury of the past. As opportunities for women are increasing, they are moving to other fields with better pay and better working hours.

The arranged marriage

One of the most painful moments for a woman who is ready for marriage is the "inspection" by the prospective groom's family. Traditionally, the man is invited to the woman's home to view her. He comes with the elders of his family.

The woman is dressed up prettily and the man's people are fed all kinds of delicious food, the parents of the woman proudly proclaiming that "our daughter has made all this with her own hands." She is brought in to be "looked at." If the man likes her, the parents discuss how much dowry is to be paid by the woman's father.

If the man rejects the woman or the dowry negotiations fall through, then the entire process begins once again. It is traumatic for a woman to know she has been rejected either because of her dark complexion (a fair complexion is highly valued) or because her father could not raise the money for her dowry.

Information about eligible men and women used to be passed by word of mouth. That still happens, but now the weekly newspaper also plays Cupid. In every Sunday newspaper, the classified advertisement pages are devoted primarily to matrimonial ads.

These ads show definite color and caste bias. All the men want a tall, fair, good-looking wife. Some of these ads now say "caste no bar," but by and large, the exact subcaste is also specified. The marriages of many young people are arranged through such ads.

Once the man and woman or the parents decide on the match, the next step is to see if the horoscopes match. A *purohit* ("poo-row-hith"), or priest, is assigned the task. If the horoscopes do not match, the marriage is called off, and the whole process begins again.

The dowry system In the Hindu community, when a woman gets married, her father has to pay a

Chote Lal's daughter

Chote Lal works as a chauffeur for a private company in Delhi. He draws a good salary—nearly $200 a month. In addition to that he has some property so he is quite well-off. He arranged a marriage for his youngest daughter, Mona, in 1992. It was a lavish affair and he spent over $5,000 just on the wedding festivities.

Mona is a working woman. She has a good job as a secretary that pays her $150 a month. Soon after she was married, her husband told her that in their family it was the custom for the wife to hand over her pay to the in-laws. Without protest, Mona gave her check to him. When she asked him for some of her own money for expenses, he gave her $5. She protested and asked for more. Her husband refused. This situation dragged on for six months. Mona, who had been independent before marriage, could not put up with his arbitrary behavior. Six months after the wedding, she was back home.

Her father has had several discussions with his son-in-law, but with no success. Mona now refuses to go back to her husband's house. She believes that if she does, the family will burn her, and her husband will marry some other unsuspecting woman.

Mona had the courage to leave her husband's home and run her life the way she wants to. Others are not so lucky. Most parents do not let a married daughter stay with them for long. In spite of all the abuse, they keep sending their daughter back to her husband's house. Any family that keeps a married daughter at home is looked down upon by society. The implication is that the woman must be "bad" if the husband does not want her. Once she is tortured or burned to death, it is too late.

substantial amount of money to the man's father in addition to several other items. Demands include gold, silver, cars, motor scooters, bicycles, washing machines, televisions, and other modern conveniences.

When the dowry system was started, it was meant to give the new bride a certain status and economic independence in her husband's home. Today the system has degenerated to such an extent that women are abused over the amount of the dowry and even killed so that the man can marry again and get another dowry. Social service organizations have been fighting relentlessly against this practice.

The pernicious dowry system is more prevalent in the North than in the South. Even educated men succumb to greed. When confronted, these men wave their hands helplessly, saying, "What is to be done? The elders wanted it this way!"

Among poor villagers, the man's parents might ask for something as humble as a bicycle, but even that is an exorbitant demand for those who do not know where their next meal will come from.

Even after the dowry demands have been met, there is no guarantee that the marriage will work. The man wants more, and more, and more.... Women are often harassed for more money or goods like a television, motor scooter, or refrigerator. If the woman's father does not pay up, she is often burned to death by her in-laws, usually with the connivance of her husband.

The government has stepped in and established an anti-dowry commission for all complaints about dowry harassment. There is recourse to courts now, and although the process seems interminably slow, there have been convictions. In one case, the offenders were sentenced to death.

The evil practice of sati

In September 1987, the country was rocked by an event that shocked progressive people. In Deorala, a village in Rajasthan, a young married woman, Roop Kanwar, only 18, was reported to have committed *sati*.

Sati was once widely practiced by Rajput women of Rajasthan. The Rajputs were the ruling princely class. In the 20th century, the practice was almost unheard of. That is why when Roop Kanwar's *sati* story broke, the nation was shaken. What was more disturbing was the fact that many responsible people, particularly politicians, glorified Roop Kanwar and her act of *sati*.

> Roop Kanwar, it is reported, was reluctant to throw herself on the burning logs, but was drugged and then dragged to the pyre. Charges were filed against her family and her in-laws.

A shrine to a woman who committed *sati*. Though illegal, *sati* is still practiced in some states.

Widowhood

"Long may you remain married," is how a bride is blessed. Therefore it is not surprising that society is particularly harsh on widows. Pandita Ramabai wrote of the plight of the Hindu widow towards the end of the 19th century:

"Throughout India widowhood is regarded as the punishment for horrible crimes committed by the woman in her former existence. But it is the child widow upon whom in an especial manner falls the abuse and hatred of the community. ... Among the Brahmans of the Deccan the heads of all widows must be shaved every fortnight. The widow must wear a single coarse garment. She must eat only one meal during the 24 hours of a day. She must never take part in family feasts. A man or woman thinks it unlucky to behold a widow's face before seeing any other object in the morning. ... Her life, then ... void of all hope, empty of every pleasure and social advantage, becomes intolerable, a curse to herself and to society at large." That was the situation prevalent even until the 1930s.

In Benares, there are many widows' homes. Discarded by their family, the widows' plight is pathetic. They gather mornings and evenings in temples to sing *bhajans* (bheh-JAHNS"), or hymns. For this, they are paid a pittance.

That situation, fortunately, is disappearing fast. Most of Rukmini Devi

Domestic abuse

On February 25, 1993, in Karnataka, Rukumavva's husband came home drunk and demanded freshly made rice. She screamed at him, "Where will I get it from if you squander it all on liquor? You may as well pour some kerosene on me and set me on fire!" The husband did precisely that. A burning Rukumavva ran out of the house, howling.

Arundale's dance development work, for example, was done after she lost her husband. In cities, particularly, no one pays much attention to the fact that a woman is a widow. Working women continue to work. Those who have not worked and have suddenly become widows, seek work.

Women power

In 1992, ordinary, rural women from the state of Andhra Pradesh realized that unless they took things into their own hands and prodded the municipal governments through demonstrations, men would continue to drink and abuse their wives. Through their actions these women changed their lives and those of rural women in other states who were inspired by them.

One of the biggest problems women face is the drunkenness of their men. The children may not have milk to drink or two square meals a day, but the men will spend their precious earnings on liquor. And liquor is easily available even in states like Gujarat and Tamil Nadu where there is prohibition.

Sale of liquor brings in a lot of revenue to the government. During elections, politicians hand out liquor bottles for votes. To satisfy this ever-growing demand, there are hundreds of liquor vendors in the country. There is at least one liquor store in most villages. Most of these sell bad-quality, cheap, locally brewed alcohol called *arrack* ("air-rack"), which is bought by men whenever they have money, such as on payday. After drinking, they come home and demand rich food. Wives simply do not have the money to buy food like that, having barely enough for the needs of the family. Then the men beat their wives and abuse them.

Incidents like this used to be all too common, not just in isolated pockets but all over the country, particularly in rural areas.

The rural women of Andhra Pradesh who were already involved in the government's literacy campaign suddenly realized they had power. They picketed

Shakti—the manifestation of female energy

In Vedic times—the era when gods and goddesses ruled the earth according to the Vedas, the holy scriptures of the Hindus—women enjoyed equal status with men. They were consorts and as such had the right to express their will and desire. Shakti was the consort of Shiva the destroyer. Shakti means power. Shakti appears in many forms. She is Durga, Kali, Sati, and Parvati. Sati and Parvati are the gentler expressions of the same Shakti. When she appears as goddesses Durga or Kali, she can both create and destroy. She can bestow favors, intercede on behalf of someone, or even take on the task of setting things right. In her incarnation as Durga, she slays Mahisasura, the demon who was causing great havoc in the world.

A woman, whether mother, sister, or wife, is regarded as the manifestation of Shakti. She may not have equal rights but is respected. Excavations at the prehistoric site of the c. 2000–5000 B.C. Indus Valley civilization suggest that the female form was venerated. That is one of the reasons for the existence of the matriarchal family.

Opposite: Widows are not supposed to wear the armfuls of bangles that is one of the symbols of a married woman.

Left: A common pictorial representation of Durga, one of the manifestations of Shakti.

Above: Rural women are champions of the environment because it is so important to their livelihood.

Right: Women working on a tea platation.

liquor stores and held demonstrations to get the government to listen to them. In the process, they managed to get liquor stores in their areas to close down. Needless to say, they were threatened by their husbands and brothers as well as by the liquor barons, but there was strength in unity.

So strong is the anti-liquor movement started by the women of Andhra Pradesh that women in other states have found the courage to join hands and fight the liquor lobby.

Women and the Environment

In rural areas, survival depends on the environment. This is particularly true for women. Most villages do not have running water. They do not have liquefied petroleum gas or kerosene, and some villages have no electricity.

Arranging to get water and fuel for the family is work for women and children. Women trudge miles for three pots of water. They make similar excursions over vast distances for firewood for cooking and fodder for their animals.

That is why women try hard to preserve the environment.

In 1977, some men entered the forests of Chamoli district of Uttar Pradesh and began to chop down the trees. The men of the village were at work and would not return until late evening. It was an ideal time for doing something illegal.

The women rushed out of their houses and asked them to stop the felling. Their lives depended on the well-being of that forest. When the men did not heed them, the women held hands and formed rings around the trees and hugged the trees. They told the men that they would have to kill them first before they could cut down the trees. Hugging something closely is called *chipko* ("chip-koh") in Hindi. These illiterate women who had been living there for centuries knew that if the forest went, they would soon follow. What the women of Chamoli started that day has grown into the Chipko Movement.

Two centuries before the women of Chamoli hugged trees, the Bishnoi women of Rajasthan had done the same thing. They were massacred and the trees cut down. Bishnois are vegetarians and are known to protect all life in their territory. Herds of deer mingle freely with people. The religious beliefs of the Bishnois have made them internationally famous. Live and let live is their motto.

Profiles of Women

T he women featured in this chapter come from diverse backgrounds but have several things in common—they are all strong, determined women who led independent lives; women who dedicated their lives to bettering conditions for others, whether by fighting for independence, leading the country, or improving conditions for working women.

Opposite: Indira Gandhi, India's first woman prime minister, giving a speech.

Right: The poor rural Indians, especially rural women—like this one crushing gravel— adored Indira Gandhi and returned her to the office of prime minister several times.

Indira Gandhi (1917–1984)

The little girl lined up the tin soldiers, armed to the teeth. Opposite the soldiers were the unarmed *satyagrahis* ("seht-yah-GRAH-hees"), or nonviolent freedom fighters. She made little flags and placed them in the hands of the *satyagrahis*.

Then the action began. The little girl encouraged them with shouts of *"Bharat Mata ki Jai"* ("Bhah-reth mah-THAH kee jye"), meaning long live Mother India, and *"Mahatma Gandhi zindabad"* ("zin-dah-bahd"), meaning long live Mahatma Gandhi. In the clash that followed, truth prevailed and the nonviolent, unarmed *satyagrahis* won their fight for freedom.

That girl was Indira Gandhi, who was later to become the country's first woman prime minister. She was merely re-enacting what she had seen and heard during the days when the country was fighting for independence from British rule. And she heard a lot, because both her father and grandfather were deeply involved in the struggle to free India of British rule.

Indira Priyadarshini Nehru was the daughter of Jawarharlal Nehru and Kamala Kaul Nehru and the granddaughter of Motilal

Nehru. She was born on November 19, 1917, in Allahabad, North India. The home of the Nehrus, Anand Bhavan, meaning abode of joy, was a beehive of political activity during those turbulent days before independence. Young Indira grew up absorbing everything, particularly the political talk.

From the time she was a child, Indira lived and breathed politics.

The Indian independence movement was based on *satyagraha* ("SEHT-yah-grah-hah"), or nonviolent, peaceful protest, advocated by Mohandas Karamchand Gandhi, popularly known as Mahatma Gandhi. Indira's father and grandfather were leaders of the movement, so they were often arrested by the British and put in prison. As a 4-year-old, she visited them in prison. Indira grew up viewing going to prison for India's freedom as nothing out of the ordinary.

In 1930, when Indira was 12, Gandhi launched a nationwide campaign of civil disobedience called the Salt Satyagraha. Since Indira was not allowed to take part in the movement, she formed the Vanar Sena, or Monkey Brigade, with children. Their duty was to serve the leaders as first-aid attendants, cooks, water bearers, and messengers.

A nonconventional education Indira, or Indu as she was fondly called, only went to school on and off. When she was 8 she travelled to Europe with her parents. There she met many intellectuals and political leaders. Her exposure to world politics was growing fast.

In 1934, she entered Visva-Bharati University, a cultural institution founded by the Indian writer and intellectual Rabindranath Tagore. Later she went to Somerville College, Oxford, where she exchanged views with other students from British colonies taking part in various anti-colonial and anti-Fascist campaigns.

Marriage to a childhood friend Indira returned to India in 1941. In March 1942 she married Feroze Gandhi, a Parsi, Zoroastrian by religion. She married not only out of her caste, but outside the Hindu religion. Feroze and Indira had been childhood friends and later fellow students at Oxford. Both Indira and Feroze went to prison several times during the struggle for independence. When she was released, she sometimes worked under the personal direction of Mahatma Gandhi.

Independence at last August 1947 brought the euphoria of independence, but also the anguish of Partition (the separation of Pakistan from India). Partition caused one of the greatest migrations in world history, with Muslims moving to the new Pakistan and Hindus moving from Pakistan to India. Millions of people lost their lives in the violence that ensued.

When Jawaharlal Nehru became the first prime minister of independent India, Indira Gandhi moved with him into the official residence of the prime minister and became his official hostess, her mother having died several years previously.

One of the most shattering memories for Indira was the assassination of Mahatma Gandhi by a Hindu fanatic in 1948. The whole country mourned for the Father of the Nation. Indira had lost not only a great teacher and guide, but a friend as well.

Steps into politics During Nehru's years as prime minister, Indira was always by his side, learning the art of politics and diplomacy. Her family grew. She had two sons, Rajiv, who was to become prime minister after her, and Sanjay. Feroze Gandhi developed his own political career and won a seat in Parliament.

In 1959, Indira was elected president of the Congress Party for one year. In 1962, China and India clashed in a war that was disastrous for India. Nehru, who had thought China was a good friend of India, was deeply disillusioned by the

Three generations of prime ministers—Indira with her father and son Rajiv at the prime minister's residence. Jawarhalal Nehru was India's first prime minister, Indira the country's first woman prime minister, and Rajiv succeeded his mother as prime minister.

Indira with her son Sanjay, whom she was grooming to succeed her. This dream never materialized, however, as Sanjay was killed in a glider crash.

In her first year as prime minister, Indira had to deal with many domestic problems of crisis proportions, such as a major food shortage. She tackled and alleviated these problems with great astuteness. Her popularity with the people grew.

Toward a secular India Indira Gandhi's passion was secularism. She wanted the Congress Party to have a secularist and socialist image. Her first opportunity for realizing this came in 1967.

Sarvepalli Radhakrishnan, the president, retired that year. Next in line for the office of president was Zakir Husain, a Muslim intellectual. Many hardline Hindus opposed Zakir Husain's nomination simply because he was Muslim. Indira was determined that he would be president.

The political battle lines were drawn. Indira staked all her personal power and prestige, as well as her office behind Zakir, and the gamble paid off. Zakir was elected president of India.

Having won one battle, Indira found herself saddled with a party that was unable to cope with the drastic problems facing India. There was ominous dissatisfaction and unrest among the people. In July 1969, she nationalized banking because small banks were charging exorbitant interest rates. The move was one that gained Indira much popularity with Indians. In August that year, her candidate for president, V.V.

Chinese attack. After that, his health deteriorated rapidly. Throughout his illness, Indira never left her father's side. On May 27, 1964, Jawaharlal Nehru, first prime minister of India, died. Feroze Gandhi had already died in 1960.

Nehru was succeeded as prime minister by Lal Bahadur Shastri. Indira became minister for information and broadcasting after having won election to Parliament.

During her term, she worked very hard to modernize and streamline the working of the bureaucracy.

Prime Minister Gandhi Lal Bahadur Shastri died in early January 1966. He was succeeded by Indira Gandhi. Soon after, she visited Britain, Russia, and the United States. She was the first woman head of government ever to visit Washington.

Giri, was elected. The Congress Party then openly split in two, as many felt that Indira was politicizing the office of the president. A number of congressmen formally joined the parliamentary opposition.

In March 1971, elections were held ahead of schedule. So great was the people's love for Indira that she was swept to a landslide victory.

Bangladesh comes into being Although victory came her way, she still had many problems. In December 1971, West Pakistan attacked India because of India's support of East Pakistani Sheikh Mujibur Rehman, who had won the elections in Pakistan fairly. India defeated Pakistan and East Pakistan declared independence, becoming the new nation of Bangladesh.

The balance of power in the subcontinent now tilted in India's favor with Bangladesh becoming India's new friend. Prime Minister Gandhi had triumphed again.

Meanwhile, Indira consolidated ties with the Societ Union. The two countries remained good political friends until the breakup of the Soviet Union.

Problems at home Although Indira Gandhi had won the elections of 1971, her political opponent, Raj Narain, filed suit against her, claiming that she had used unfair means to win the election. In 1975, judgment was delivered in favor of Narain. It disqualified Indira from holding office for six years.

While the opposition went on a celebration spree, Indira, fully convinced that if she were out of office it would be harmful for the nation, declared a state of emergency. The 19 months that followed were dark days for Indian democracy. In the next election, Indira Gandhi was defeated.

She was back in power within two years, however, because the opposition parties forming the government spent a lot of time fighting each other, so nothing got done. The country was

Standing straight

India was one of the leaders of the nonaligned movement. Although India had close diplomatic ties with the Soviet Union, Indira Gandhi saw no reason why India should cut itself off from the United States and the Western bloc. Following in her father's footsteps, she threw herself into the activities of the nonaligned movement.

During her visit to the White House in the early 1980s, Indira was asked by one of the members of the press whether India would lean toward the United States or the Soviet Union. Looking the reporter straight in the eye, she said, "India as always will stand straight. I see no reason for her to lean either way."

facing many crises. The electorate, fed up with inefficiency, wanted Indira back. And back she came with a resounding victory.

But she never regained the brilliance that had characterized her previous years in office. Her son Sanjay, whom she had been grooming to take over from her, died tragically in a glider crash. Punjab was in turmoil, with Sikh militants demanding a separate country. Thousands of people were killed and Hindus were fleeing Punjab.

In June 1984, Indira ordered military forces into the Sikhs' most holy shrine, the Golden Temple at Amritsar, to flush out the militants who were running a campaign of terrorism from there. This one single event, Operation Blue Star, eventually cost Indira her life. On October 31, 1984, she was assassinated by her own Sikh bodyguard.

When Indians remember Indira Gandhi, it is not her mistakes that come to mind. They remember a warm woman, adored by people who believed she could do no wrong. She was one of them. She ate with them, slept with them, wept with them. She shared their sorrows and their joys. She was, more than anything else, *amma* ("ehm-mah"), or mother. For the intelligentsia, she was a prime minister one was proud to have. She could converse with prime ministers and presidents with ease and conviction. She never gave an inch if she felt it was a wrong decision. She was a woman who felt she had to do the best for her country and her people.

Raziya Sultan (d. 1240)

Raziya Sultan succeeded to the throne of the Delhi Sultanate in spite of the fact that she had brothers. Her father Iltutmish (1211–1236), the first sultan of Delhi, decided to nominate Raziya to rule after him as he felt that his sons were not capable of administration.

Not a sultana

Raziya was an excellent ruler, better than most sultans. In fact, she objected to being called "Raziya Sultana" as it was the title used by the wife of a sultan. That is why she is called Raziya Sultan.

She was not, however, destined to enjoy a peaceful reign. Raziya had a trusted Abyssinian slave, Jalal-ud-din Yaqut. She elevated him to the post of master of the stables. This offended the Turkish nobles. There are conflicting reports on her closeness to Jalal-ud-din. A writer says, "A very great degree of familiarity was observed to exist between the Abyssinian and the Queen, so much so that when she rode, he always lifted her onto her horse by raising her up under the arms."

But who wants to be ruled over by a woman? After Iltutmish's death, the nobles of his court disregarded his wishes. They placed Iltutmish's eldest surviving son, Rukn-ud-din Firuz, on the throne instead.

Rukn and his ambitious mother proceeded to squander the wealth of the kingdom. The whole kingdom was plunged into disorder. The nobles of Delhi imprisoned mother and son and placed Raziya on the throne of Delhi.

A young queen takes charge The task before young Razia Sultan was not an easy one. Many of the nobles who still resented the rule of a woman organized a revolt against her. But Raziya had all the astuteness and diplomacy required in a ruler and she soon overpowered her enemies. She declared herself queen of Hindustan and Punjab. The governors of the distant provinces of Bengal and Sindh also acknowledged her rule.

Many were still outraged at being ruled by a woman. The first to revolt openly was Ikhtiyar-ud-din Altuniya, governor of Sarhind. The queen marched with a large army to suppress the revolt, but in the ensuing conflict the rebels slew the faithful Jalal and imprisoned Raziya. She was placed in Ikhtiyar's custody and her brother Mu'iz-ud-din Bahram was proclaimed sultan of Delhi.

Raziya very cleverly tried to make the best of a bad situation by marrying

Ikhtiyar, but it was of no use. She marched with her husband toward Delhi but was defeated on October 13, 1240 by her brother. Together with her husband Ikhtiyar, she was put to death the next day. The first woman sultan had been in power for only a little over three years.

A remarkable woman Raziya was a remarkably talented woman. One writer called her a great sovereign, sagacious, just, and beneficent; a patron of the learned, a dispenser of justice, the cherisher of her subjects. he also admired her warlike talent and though her endowed with all the admirable attributes and qualifications necessary for kings.

Raziya fought like a man and led her troops into battle herself. She broke all accepted codes by discarding the *burqah*. She even donned the tunic and assumed the headdress of a man.

Her *durbars* ("derh-bars"), or congregations to hear petitions, were held in the open. She attempted to be the king at all times. Raziya Sultan's story clearly shows that it is not easy to overcome popular prejudices.

Mira was unable to understand why her husband could not appreciate her god. One reason was that the *bhaktas* ("bhehk-tahs") or mendicants she moved with were not all from the upper castes. Devotees were all equal in the eyes of the Lord. Mira asks her husband:

Rana, why are you my enemy?
You seem the *karil* ("kah-ril"—thorny acacia tree) among trees to me.
I left your palace, and your roof; I left your city.
I stopped putting on *kajal* ("kah-jehl"—kohl) and beauty spots, and put on sash and shawl (ascetic robes).
Mira's lord is Giridhar Nagar (Krishna).
He turned the poison to nectar.

(trans. Zide and Pandey, from Mirabai ki Padavali *by Parshuram Chaturvedi, 17th edition, 1983, Hindi Sahitya Sammelan, Allahabad)*

Mirabai (c. 1504–c. 1550)

Mirabai was a great saint-poet of North India, but she is also revered and loved throughout the country. She composed some beautiful *bhajans* (songs) in praise of the god Krishna.

Mirabai was born into a Rajput or warrior family of Mewar in Rajasthan in a small fort at Kudki. No one knows the exact date of her birth, but it was around 1504.

As a young child, Mira wanted to know the meaning of the word *bridegroom*. She was told that every girl has a

> "One's name will live on through one's work, consider this if you are wise; Mira did not give birth to a son nor did she have any disciples."
> *Popular saying*

bridegroom. Mira then wanted to know who her bridegroom was. To escape Mira's incessant questioning, her mother pointed to the image of the dark god Krishna, telling her he was her bridegroom. Mira fell instantly in love with the god and from then on considered herself the bride of Lord Krishna.

Marriage She was married into the royal family of Sisodia Rajputs of Mewar. No one knows for certain who her husband was. Some say it was Maharana Kumbh. Scholars believe that she was married to Bhojraj, eldest son of the famed warrior Rana Sanga.

According to legend, when Mira reached her husband's home, she was taken to worship the family deity, the goddess Devi. Mira refused. She was, after all, married to Lord Krishna. Her mother-in-law was furious and told her son to get rid of Mira. "She has insulted me. Why wait for further evidence?"

Most women would have broken under the pressure. Not Mira. She refused to fall into the mold of a conforming, unquestioning *bahu* ("bah-hoo"), or daughter-in-law. And contrary to all traditions of Rajasthan, she refused to consummate her marriage as she was already married to Lord Krishna. She defied convention and associated with male *bhaktas* who were worshipers of Lord Krishna.

Her love for her god took her to many places of worship. There she sang and danced in joyous abandon. This was not behavior expected of a Rajput princess.

How did Mira die? Legend says that Mira was staying at the Ranchhorji temple in Dwarka, Gujarat. At that time, messengers came to her from her mother's as well as her husband's family asking her to return. She refused. She was happy. Why should she get involved in all the hassles of domestic life? The messengers, all belonging to the Brahmin class, said they would fast unto death outside the temple if she did not return with them.

If the Brahmins died, their blood would be on Mira's head. She prayed hard, asking Lord Krishna to save her. Then she entered the temple and disappeared! Some say that she was absorbed into the image of Lord Krishna. Others say that she walked out of the back door into the sea. But no one knows what really happened to Mira.

Mira started no mass movements. But for the individual, she was a great source of inspiration and strength. Her songs are eminently singable and convey a joyous sense of abandon.

Gandhi and Mira Gandhi often referred to Mira in his speeches. She was the symbol of gentle resistance to tyranny and injustice. In Mira's resistance to her husband was all the philosophy of *satyagraha*.

Mirabai singing and dancing in ecstasy before her beloved Lord Krishna.

Turning poison into nectar

Mira's husband was taunted by others about his wayward wife. Angry and humiliated, he decided to poison her. He sent her a cup of poison. She drank it without a murmur. Krishna had turned it into nectar! This incident is repeated over and over in her songs.

I'm colored with the color of dusk, O Rana
colored with the color of my Lord.
Drumming out the rhythm on the drums I danced,
dancing in the presence of the saints,
colored with the color of my Lord.
The rana sent me a poison cup:
I didn't look, I drank it up,
colored with the color of my Lord.

Her husband did not stop with the poisoned cup. Mirabai in her songs tells of the many ways the rana tried to kill her. But Krishna saved her every time. Her husband sent her a serpent in a basket, but it turned into the image of her god; a bed of thorns changed into a bed of flowers when she lay on it.

Gandhi often compared Mira to Socrates. Both were offered a cup of poison. Both drank without fear or rancor.

He saw in Mira's life an expression of a woman's individuality which is suppressed throughout her life. He believed that a man had no right to compel his wife to do anything she disliked just because her husband wants her to do it!

Gandhi wrote, "A Hindu husband seems to think that a wife is a chattel. I have heard monster-like husbands referring to the wives as their property. ... Does not the wife have an individuality too? Damayanti had it. Mirabai showed that she too had it." Gandhi wanted women to look to Mira as a role model, and men to see her husband as a negative role model.

The many moods of Mira Mira symbolizes different things to different people. To some she was a mystic, lost in her devotion to god. To others she was an anti-establishment rebel who fought against domination by her husband and his family.

The latter view is particularly prominent in the Rajput community to which she belonged. Rajputs pride themselves on their valor and their women, whom they keep mainly hidden. If a woman did something out of the ordinary, it cast a shadow on their honor. After all, the woman belonged to them. How dare she make an exhibition of herself?

The Rajputs sanctioned *sati* and *jauhar* ("JOW-her")—community immolation by women who believed that their husbands either had died or would die in battle. Mira made total mockery of those who expended time and energy zealously guarding their women's sexual virtue. She is an extraordinary figure. She did not belong to any rebellion or movement. She was simply her own individual self.

Laxmibai, rani of Jhansi (1835–1858)

On November 19, 1835, a girl was born to Moropant and Bhagirathibai of Kashi (now Varanasi, previously Benares). She was named Manikarnika but was called Manu. Manu's mother died when she was 4 years old.

Moropant joined the court of the exiled *peshwa* ("paysh-wah"), or ruler, Bajirao II. Manu grew up playing with Bajirao's adopted son, Nana Dhondu Pant, who was later known as Nana Saheb. Unlike other girls, Manu showed no interest in dolls.

Children learn about the legendary courage of Rani Laxmibai of Jhansi in school.

A young girl dressed up as Laxmibai in a re-enactment of the battle at Jhansi.

Nana Saheb complained of severe aches and pains. Manu said, "How can you be a great warrior if you can't put up with the slightest pain?"

Tying the knot Soon her marriage to Raja Gangadhar Rao of Jhansi was arranged. The ceremony took place at the Ganesha Temple outside Jhansi. The aged priest had trouble tying the ceremonial knot, and Manu said to the priest, "Tie a knot that will never open."

After the wedding Manu was renamed Laxmibai. A son was born to them, but he died in three months.

The British wanted to annex Jhansi as the ruler did not have a male heir. So the couple adopted a young boy. Laxmibai's husband died soon after, and Laxmibai became a widow when she was only 18.

Before his death, the raja had written to the British governor-general, Lord Dalhousie, asking him to be kind to his adopted son and to allow the state to be governed by his adoptive mother "during the length of her life."

The British would have none of it, however. Laxmibai was more than competent to rule, but they had set their minds on annexing Jhansi. Laxmibai was awarded a life pension of $2,400. She was allowed to keep the palace but had to give up the fort. The adopted heir, when he came of age, would be allowed to inherit the raja's personal estate but not the throne.

Not like other girls With the boys, Manu began to learn swordsmanship, shooting, riding, and even wrestling. She soon was proficient in all of them.

Many stories of Manu's bravery as a child have been passed down from generation to generation.

Once, in a horse race between her and Nana Saheb, Manu had already gone ahead when Nana had a heavy fall. So many people fussed over him that Manu became quite contemptuous.

"I shall not surrender!" Laxmibai did not want money. She wanted her beloved Jhansi. "I shall not surrender my Jhansi!" she declared passionately. She issued an appeal to the Court of Directors in London. The appeal was rejected. Then she was told she would have to pay her late husband's debts out of her own pension. That angered her further.

This was also a time of great discontent all over North India. Several rulers were planning revolts. It is said that Laxmibai joined them. She displayed military acumen by proposing a simultaneous outbreak of several revolts starting May 31, 1857. This would give the British no time to recoup or transfer forces. This plan was accepted unanimously.

But before systematic preparations could be made, the Sepoy Revolt began on May 6, 1857, at Meerut. A number of sepoys seized the Meerut garrison.

News of the Meerut revolt spread rapidly. What Laxmibai feared had come to pass. After the Meerut revolt was suppressed, a number of rebels turned on the British at Jhansi. The British turned to Laxmibai for help. She was unable to help and many British soldiers were massacred. This was called the Jhansi massacre.

Laxmibai wrote to Major W.C. Erskine and explained her inability to help the British. She expressed her regret at the massacre. Erskine believed her, but the colonial administration at Calcutta did not. As a result of this, when Jhansi was attacked by two neighboring states, the British ignored her appeals for help.

Laxmibai then took matters into her own hands. She called up her army and rode out to battle on horseback. She led her troops and finally repelled the invaders.

There is a poem in Hindi that every school child recites. Translated, the refrain reads:
She fought like a warrior
She fought like a tiger;
There was no other
Like the queen of Jhansi.

Taking on the British Even at that point, Laxmibai had no intention of fighting the British. But when she heard that the formidable British army was on its way to avenge the massacre at Jhansi, she decided she had no option but to fight.

The huge army appeared and laid siege to Jhansi on March 21, 1858. In command was Sir Hugh Rose. For the next 10 days his infantry fired ceaselessly upon the forces manning the ramparts. Laxmibai had marshaled her troops well. She involved women too, using them to carry ammunition to the batteries. Her intention was to hold out until a relieving force led by Tatya Tonpe arrived.

But on March 30, the fort wall was breached through a collaborator's treachery. Laxmibai erected a stockade that kept the English at bay.

Meanwhile Tatya Tonpe arrived but was quickly routed. On April 2, Rose began his sustained assault on Jhansi fort. Laxmibai was reluctant to leave but was persuaded by her soldiers to beat a strategic retreat to fight another day.

She took an escort of soldiers and rode away to Kalpi. The British troops overtook them at Banda, 20 miles away, and a fierce fight began. Laxmibai fought her way through and reached Kalpi. The British followed her on to Kalpi only to find nobody there.

> **After the fight at Banda, an awed British officer of the 3rd Bombay Light Cavalry said of Laxmibai, "She is a wonderful woman, very brave and determined. It is fortunate for us that the men are not all like her."**

Meanwhile, Tatya Tonpe's army had fled. The rebels were dispirited and began to bicker, the cavalry and infantry blaming each other.

At this point the rani, accompanied by Rao Sahib, a nephew of Nana Saheb, arrived. She rallied the rebels and led them back to Kalpi. She pleaded passionately with them to defeat the *firingis* ("feh-RING-geez"), meaning foreigners, or die gloriously in the attempt.

On May 22, Laxmibai led the attack. A grim battle followed and the rebels had to retreat. It seemed to the British that the war was over. But Laxmibai drew up a bold plan. She marched on Gwalior, an ally of the British. The maharaja of Gwalior opposed them, but after firing one round, his guns were captured. His army went over to the rebels, forcing the maharaja to flee.

Rose, who had been planning his vacation, now had to change his plans. On June 17, his forces clashed with the Indian rebels led by Laxmibai. It was this final battle that consolidated the legend of Laxmibai of Jhansi.

On horseback, with her young son tied to her back and sword in hand, the rani fought fiercely. A British observer remarked that she fought "using her sword with both hands and holding the reins of her horse in her mouth." Her astounding bravery was of no avail. The legendary and courageous Laxmibai of Jhansi was killed on the battlefield.

There are conflicting reports about her death but the most widely accepted one is based on a report in Lord Canning's papers. It said that she was shot in the back by a trooper of the 8th Hussars.

Legend has it that Laxmibai, though fatally wounded, turned around and ran her sword through the trooper. Then she managed to break away and reach a nearby hut with one of her soldiers. Before dying she made the man promise to cremate her instantly so that no foreigner would touch her.

Sarojini Naidu (1879–1949)

She was called the "Nightingale of India" by Mahatma Gandhi because of her poetry. But Sarojini was also a freedom fighter, a writer, a politician, and an administrator.

Sarojini Chattopadhyay was born on February 13, 1879, 10 years after Mahatma Gandhi. Her family were Bengali Brahmins from Hyderabad. Her father was well-versed in several foreign languages—English, Hebrew, German, and Russian—and was the founder-principal of the New Hyderabad College. Her mother was deeply interested in poetry and music. So Sarojini, in her early years, was exposed to both the arts and the sciences.

The Chattopadhyays were liberal, broadminded, and deeply influenced by the reform movements sweeping the country, in particular the Brahmo Samaj (see page 24).

Love of poetry Even as a young girl, Sarojini wrote poetry and kept diaries. When she was 12, she was sent to Madras to complete the public high school exams. She passed with first-class honors. In 1896, her father published a collection of her poems.

Around this time, she fell ill as a

result of overwork. The doctor ordered her not to touch a book. So she wrote a 2000-line play *Meher Munir*. She sent a copy to the *nizam* ("nee-zahm"), or ruler, of Hyderabad. The *nizam* was so moved by it that he gave her an annual scholarship of $800 to study in Britain.

In England, Sarojini spent most of her time writing poetry. Literary scholars like Edmund Gosse and Arthur Simmons began to notice her. Eventually William Heinemann published three collections of her poetry, *The Golden Threshold* (1905), *The Bird of Time* (1912)

Sarojini Naidu worked closely with Mahatma Gandhi in the independence movement.

and *The Broken Wing* (1917). These three works established Sarojini as the most important Indian poet after Rabindranath Tagore.

She returned to India in 1898 and married Dr. Govind Rajulu Naidu, with whom she had fallen in love before leaving for England. They were married in a civil ceremony as this was an inter-caste marriage. Soon after her marriage, she became interested in women's issues and became an active member of the women's movement.

From women's issues, it was only a small step to politics. In 1905, she openly denounced the British policies of exploitation.

Sarojini was a great liberal thinker. She was not influenced by the divisions of caste or religion. She felt people were all the same—all human beings. In 1906, at the Calcutta session of the Indian National Congress, she made an impassioned speech in which she exhorted the people to think of themselves not as Hindus or Muslims but as Indians.

Sarojini meets Gandhi

Sarojini's health was generally poor. Once again, in 1912, illness kept her away from her work. She was sent to England for medical treatment, and that was where she met Mahatma Gandhi for the first time.

When Sarojini first saw him, he was sitting on a coarse black blanket spread on the floor and eating mashed tomatoes with some dry *chapatis* ("cheh-PAH-tees"), or Indian unleavened bread. She was so amused by the sight that she burst out laughing. Gandhi, who did not know her at all, merely smiled and said, "You must be Sarojini Naidu. No one else would dare laugh at me." After this Sarojini began a unique relationship with Mahatma Gandhi.

Sarojini was perhaps the only person who, though genuinely in awe of Gandhi, could take liberties with him. Gandhi had a special diet. As a vegetarian, he ate almonds and honey and drank goat's milk. Sarojini is once reported to have teased him, saying, "Do you know how much it costs to keep you poor?"

In England, Sarojini organized the Indian student movement. She was fully convinced that the future of the country lay with the young. In his autobiography, Jawaharlal Nehru recollects her stirring speeches, unmatched as far as nationalism and patriotism went.

Working towards freedom

On her return to India Sarojini threw herself completely into the freedom movement. Of what use was a country if one had to live under the foreign yoke? Along with Dr. Annie Besant, she toured all the major towns of the country, exhorting people to stand up for an independent India.

Sarojini Naidu was at the forefront of all the major nationalist movements. She was part of the Home Rule Move-

ment, organizing the exploited indigo farmers of Champaran. She joined in the protests against the Rowlatt Act, which severely curtailed the freedom of the press in an attempt to limit public knowledge of the independence movement, and other British policies.

People make much of returning awards today. But as early as 1920 Sarojini returned the *Kesar-i-Hind*, a title awarded to her by the British, feeling that she could not accept an award from a country that was exploiting her people. By now, Sarojini was a complete Gandhian, though she could still be critical of him.

Like Gandhi, Sarojini believed in nonviolence as a weapon to win freedom. So when Gandhi launched the noncooperation movement, Sarojini Naidu was one of its most enthusiastic leaders.

When Gandhi was arrested, he called Sarojini before leaving for prison. He told her, "The fortunes of India are now in your hands."

The British often tried to set one community against another. They also used excessive force to suppress riots, regardless of the sex and age of the participants. Sarojini publicly condemned the British government for these vile practices. The British government demanded that Sarojini either apologize

Sarojini Naidu was deeply involved in the women's movement and encouraged women to fight for their rights.

Sarojini Naidu
accepts flowers
from an admirer.

excerpting her speech, likened her to Joan of Arc.

In 1928, Sarojini represented India at the World Women's Conference in Honolulu. In 1929, she was a part of the five-member conference—the others being Gandhi, Motilal Nehru (Indira Gandhi's grandfather), Muhammed Ali Jinnah (founder of Pakistan), and Sardar Vallabhbhai Patel (another Indian nationalist)—that met with Lord Curzon to discuss the possibility of awarding India self-rule. The talks fell through. The demand was now for complete independence.

Fighting unfair laws One of the most memorable events of the freedom movement was the march against the salt tax, called the Dandi March. On April 6, 1930, Sarojini was alongside Gandhi on the march. When Gandhi was arrested, it was Sarojini who kept the march going.

Despite brutal attacks by the police, Sarojini managed to keep the march nonviolent. The men would move forward, only to be struck down by the police. Then the women would remove them for first-aid. Then the next lot would step forward only to be clubbed. Over 300 such volunteers were injured. Finally Sarojini was arrested.

Sarojini was arrested time and again. When she was arrested again in 1940, the authorities released her when they saw she was in poor health. She wrote,

or face the consequences. Sarojini, of course, flatly refused to back down.

From 1922 to 1926 Sarojini placed India's nationalist cause and women's movement before various international conferences. With such a proven track record, it was no surprise that at the 1925 Kanpur session of the INC, Gandhi nominated her president. She was elected unanimously. Her acceptance speech was a landmark in public speaking. *The New York Times*,

"I have been so summarily released because they fear that I may die among my beloved flowers." This was a reference to the prison gardens that she used to tend.

Quit India Movement ... and after
After 1941 the independence movement intensified and almost all the top leaders were imprisoned. Sarojini took on the responsibility of the kitchen in prison. On her release in 1945, Sarojini threw herself into the Quit India Movement, a branch of the independence movement. She was also confronted with the additional grief of her son's death.

Freedom at midnight India became independent on August 15, 1947, at the stroke of midnight. The cost was terrible. The country was partitioned; there were riots and mass migrations.

Sarojini took over the governorship of Uttar Pradesh while the incumbent governor was recuperating from an illness. When the governor returned and saw how efficiently Sarojini was running the state, he promptly handed in his resignation, saying that Uttar Pradesh could have no better governor. Sarojini Naidu thus became the country's first woman governor.

By 1949 Sarojini's health began failing again, but she resolutely kept at her work. In February 1949, she fell seriously ill after her return to Lucknow from an official visit to Delhi. Even with an oxygen mask, she found it difficult to breathe. On the night of March 1, she asked her nurse to sing her favorite hymn, "Jesu, Lover of my Soul." Midway through the rendition, Sarojini died. Her birthday, February 13, is celebrated as Indian Women's Day.

Ela Bhatt (b. 1933)

Ela Bhatt is a household name today, especially in the western state of Gujarat. But for her, the women of Gujarat would continue to be exploited. And, like countless women all over India, they would have endured everything in silence.

Ela Bhatt gave them a newfound confidence. Because of Ela, the women know they can organize themselves into working groups. SEWA (Self-Employed Women's Association) means "service" in local languages. And Ela Bhatt's SEWA has indeed served the women of Gujarat.

The story of SEWA is also the story of Ela Bhatt.

Excluding women

As the textile industry went in for technological modernization, the number of women in low-skilled jobs went down. There were men working in low-skilled jobs too, but they were trained to meet the demands of the new technology. Women were not. In 1925, 25% of workers in the Ahmedabad textile industry were women. In 1975, women made up only 2.5% of the textile workforce.

"In 1972, when we started SEWA, we had no idea how to do it or where to start, but two things I saw clearly: in our country, most of the production of goods and services are done through the self-employed sector— 89% of our labor force is self-employed. Unless they are brought into the mainstream of the labor movement, it is no movement worth the name.

"Secondly, I recognized that 80% of Indian women are poor, illiterate, and economically very active. It is these working-class women who should be taking a leading role in the women's movement of our country. Ninety percent of these women's time is taken up in their work. If we bring these women into the movement on the basis of work, it is strategically the most effective way of organizing large numbers of women according to issues which are relevant to them."

Ela Bhatt, May 1988

Growing up Ela Bhatt's father and grandfather were lawyers in Surat, a coastal town of diamond merchants in Gujarat. Mahatma Gandhi was born in Gujarat. Ela's grandparents, like most intellectuals, were Mahatma Gandhi's followers and were deeply involved in the freedom movement.

Young Ela naturally grew up absorbing Gandhian principles and following the Gandhian way of life.

(Mahatma Gandhi stood for nonviolence and the empowering of the oppressed classes.) When she graduated with a law degree in 1955, she looked for work that would help tackle the problems of poverty and injustice.

As far back as 1917, another revolutionary woman, Anusuyabehn Sarabhai, together with Mahatma Gandhi, had founded the Textile Labour Association (TLA) trade union. Ela decided to join the TLA office in Ahmedabad as their lawyer in order to represent the TLA workers.

Unionizing poor working women In 1968, Ela was asked to head the TLA Women's Wing. By then she was married to Ramesh Bhatt, an activist and professor of economics. The Women's Wing only dealt with the families of textile workers. They were taught skills like sewing to supplement the family income. Ela was convinced that poor

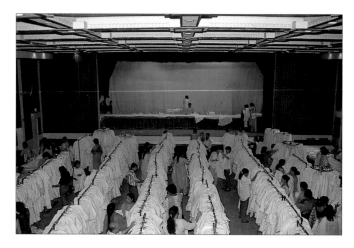

An exhibition of merchandise produced at the Lucknow SEWA garment factory.

working women who had no backing of any sort needed the help of a union.

Her chance came in 1971. Some migrant women who carried loads on their heads and pulled carts approached Ela. They had heard of her work with TLA and wanted to know if something could be done for them too. These women lived on the streets with their families. They did not even have basic amenities. They worked from morning until late at night and all they were paid was 30 cents a day. Often, policemen harassed them and they had to bribe them out of their meager earnings in order to be left alone.

Then Ela met Chanda. Chanda was a Vaghari woman. That meant she belonged to the lowest class. She lived in one of the back lanes of Ahmedabad, in an appalling slum. She was a garment dealer in used clothes. With clever repair work, she made them as good as new and sold them very cheaply in the market. She related the story of her working conditions to Ela *behn* ("bhayn," or sister).

Chanda wanted to know why she and others like her could not share some of the benefits the TLA was helping its workers to get. Ela could only find one solution. "You need to organize yourselves if you want to get some of these benefits," she said.

The birth of SEWA The first meeting of self-employed women who worked

Sheba Hussain, SEWA's account manager, checking the books.

at various trades was called. It was attended by 100 women. It was the first step. SEWA was born on December 3, 1971. Ela Bhatt was its general secretary. Since then SEWA has not looked back.

The next step was to organize credit. Banks were unwilling to lend money to the poorest of the poor, as these women were. They were a credit risk. Though Ela managed to convince bankers that poor women are not necessarily a risk, the women still had problems. Then Chanda asked, "Behn, why can't we have our own bank?"

"I saw that women everywhere are ready to take leadership. In every group we met, there were women whose eyes were burning with an inner fire. If these women are reached and encouraged, it is they who will be our future leaders."

Ela Bhatt

> "We not only want a piece of the pie, we also want to choose the flavor and know how to make it ourselves."
>
> *Ela Bhatt*

It was an exciting idea. Could it work? Would these illiterate women be able to handle all the financial dealings? Ela was able to convince the authorities that it was possible. The Mahila SEWA Sahakari Bank was established in July 1974. The night before the registration, 15 women sat up all night learning how to sign their names!

The bank faced many problems. Women did not understand the need to pay back their loan interest regularly. If one did not pay, neither did all her friends. All these problems were overcome, and today, the Mahila bank is the envy of the conventional banks. Default on payment is minimal. The women run the bank like professionals.

Mahila SEWA Trust was the next organization set up to give social security to women. It was done entirely through the donation of one day's wages by each of the workers.

In 1977, Ela received the Magsaysay Award for Community Leadership and Public Service. She donated the entire $20,000 to the trust.

Literacy was something women workers could not make time for. They were too busy earning a living. Ela says, "I knocked my head against the wall for years!" Even today, literacy for the women workers is not a top priority, but children of SEWA workers go to school.

SEWA grew slowly, absorbing more and more trades. It consisted of women from all communities: tribal women, migrants, cart-pullers, agricultural laborers, vegetable vendors, even rag pickers. Ela was the spirit holding them together.

All this while, TLA and SEWA had been affiliated. However, dissension between TLA and SEWA grew. In 1981,

> "Some unions do take up issues related to women workers, or include a women's wing in the larger body of the union, but there are very few unions in the world which are devoted entirely to a female membership, as SEWA is. SEWA organizes women who work in their homes, in the streets of cities, in the fields and villages of rural India, with no fixed employer, carving their small niches in the economy, day by day, with only their wits to guide them against incredible odds of vulnerability, invisibility, and poverty."
>
> *Kalima Rose,* Where Women are Leaders

following riots between Hindus and Muslims, TLA broke away from SEWA. It was then that SEWA acquired its female identity. Since the split, SEWA has been made up solely of women. Men are not allowed to hold office.

International recognition In 1975, Ela Bhatt attended the conference in Mexico City held for the International Women's Year. Ela spoke about the SEWA banking experience, among other things. Learning from SEWA's experience, the Women's World Banking was established in 1981. It gives credit to women worldwide who have no other access to credit.

In recognition of her services to the nation's cause in a wider sense and the women's cause in particular, Ela Bhatt was offered a seat in the upper house of Parliament in 1986.

A woman praying in the Ganges river, giving thanks for all that she has. SEWA has helped millions of poor rural women start up their own cottage industries to supplement the family income.

chapter six

A Lifetime

Families in India are close and loving. Older people are respected and their word is law. Within the family structure, the woman has different roles to play. As a daughter, she is loved and treasured by her family. Her brother always comes to her rescue if she needs help. As a wife, she is the daughter-in-law of the family. Her behavior must in no way embarrass the family. At no time can she be herself—a person with an identity, someone with hopes and longings. A woman juggles all these roles with skill and keeps the family together.

Birth

In all major communities, girls are considered a burden. Only where the matriarchal society still remains (in some parts of the southern state of Kerala, in northeast Assam, and among tribal people) is a woman regarded as an asset and not a liability. Among the Hindus, a girl is regarded as Lakshmi, the goddess of wealth; yet when a girl is born, no one comes to congratulate the family.

In poor villages in certain parts of the country, female infanticide is common. In the desert area of Rajasthan, there is a mound called *gudiyon ka tilla* ("GOOD-ee-yoh kah TILL-lah"), or the mound of dolls, near a certain hamlet. No one talks about it, but everyone knows that this is where unwanted female babies are buried. The practice of female infanticide was thought to be a phenomenon common only in

Opposite: A young girl pauses on her way to get water.

Right: A boy's birth is celebrated in India, but a girl's is, at best, ignored.

Going home to mother for the baby

Most young women go to their mother's home to give birth, especially for their first baby. They usually travel in the seventh or the ninth month of pregnancy. When they are at their mother's house, a special ceremony takes place. The mother-to-be is given an auspicious turmeric bath. Her hair is washed with herbs. It is then dried over a fire in which fragrant myrrh has been sprinkled. Her hair is parted in the center (even if it is normally parted on the side) to ensure a well-proportioned boy and to symbolically ward off shocks. Soothing instrumental music is played and holy verses are read out to her for the birth of a male child.

During her pregnancy, the mother-to-be is made to sweep and swab the floor, for which she has to bend or squat on her haunches. This exercises the muscles that will make the delivery easier. In wealthy families, the pregnant woman—always accompanied—is taken for long walks. These are the most wonderful days for a woman. There is no house to run, no husband to worry about, no responsibility of any kind, and the woman is pampered and spoiled by her parents. No wonder all pregnant women want to come home!

For 12 weeks after the baby is born, the new mother is not allowed to work at all. Her duty is only to feed the baby and look after herself. A *maalishwalli* ("mah-lish-wah-lee"), or masseuse, is engaged for the three months she stays at her parents' home after the baby is born. She is fed different things in different parts of the country, all of them intended to get her strong again to face life in her own home. In northern Punjab, the food is very heavy and rich—ghee, or clarified butter, is added to everything. Stimulating ingredients like almonds, dried fruit, and sesame seeds are soaked, ground, and eaten plain or stirred into milk. In the south, young mothers are given garlic, either deep-fried or raw, to stimulate milk production.

When the mother is fully rested after three months, she comes back home where she and the baby are welcomed with much rejoicing.

This is the scenario in a middle- or upper-class home. Where the family is poor, however, there is no such luxury as time off from work. Women who work at construction sites just go off to a secluded spot when they feel the baby coming. If they are lucky, they take another woman with them to help. If not, they do it all themselves, including the cutting of the umbilical cord, and get back to work the same day!

North India, but in 1992, Indians were astounded and horrified to find it flourishing in the southern district of Madurai as well.

In cities, people have access to amniocentesis, the process by which a child's sex can be determined very early in the pregnancy. If it is a girl, the pregnant woman is often coerced by her husband and/or parents-in-law to have an abortion. Girls make up 90% of all babies left in the cradle outside Shishu Sadan, a nursery run by the Missionaries of Charity.

Women's groups have been agitating against sex-determination clinics. The federal government has also been running a series of advertisements on television and in national newspapers to show that girls are every bit as good as boys. In fact, the family-planning commercial, which earlier showed a family of four—mother, father, a boy, and a girl—now shows only the parents and a girl. Billboards carry slogans on how important a daughter is. All this is helping, though very slowly, to change attitudes.

Daughters are traditionally treated as of less values than sons, but the government has embarked on a campaign to change this attitude.

In rural areas, boys are a family's income. They tend the sheep and goats, help till the land, and go to the market. Besides, when they marry, they bring home a dowry. Girls also help, but usually within the home. They look after their siblings, cook, and take food to the boys working in the field. But the cost of marriage, especially the dowry, makes a daughter a liability. As it is, since they have to spend so much when the girl is grown, most parents do not send their daughter to school.

Large families

One of the biggest problems is over-population. Yet if you were to ask a villager what his most important asset is, he would probably say, "Children." Large families are a symptom of extreme poverty. Since health services in villages are practically nonexistent, no one knows how many children will survive. To guard against sudden death, they have more children. To feed more children, they need more money. And when they are short of money, it is always the girls who suffer.

In many homes, particularly in Rajasthan, which is extremely backward, girls are, as a matter of course, fed less than their brothers. "What does it matter?" parents reason. "She is someone else's property anyway. Tomorrow

A family at a Hindu shrine.

The world's largest joint family

The Narasingannavar ("na-ra-sing-ahnna-vaar") family of Lokur, a place a little larger than a village, seems almost out of place and out of time. That is because at a time when the country seems to be moving toward the nuclear family, the Narasingannavars continue to add to their joint family. And what a family!

They have been living together as a joint family for the last 150 years and they now have a total of 110 members. They eat the same food and share everything. Another 50 members work outside Lokur. The head of this vast household is 65-year-old Bhimana ("bhee-ma-na"). He runs the family on strictly traditional lines. Their main occupation is farming their 200 acres of agricultural land.

The women look after the daily household chores. Work is divided among them so that each one knows what she is doing. It is a massive operation in time management. About 600 millet *rotis* ("roh-tis")—flattened bread cooked on a griddle—are made for lunch in the afternoon. To accompany this, vast quantities of *dal* ("dahl")—lentil curry—and vegetables are cooked. Since there are so many members in the family, they eat in shifts.

she will get married and go away." Such an attitude seems callous to Westerners. It is not that girls are not loved. It is simply accepted that girls and women are second-class beings and therefore do not need the same amount or the same quality of food that boys and men do. Even wealthy, urban, educated parents can be guilty of this discrimination.

In cities, however, families are getting smaller. One reason is that there is not enough space for large families. Another is that better health care is available in the city so infant mortality is not that high. More children, in fact, means more expense because families have to send them to school and see that they are cared for.

The joint family

Although the nuclear family is becoming common, the joint family still exists in small towns and rural areas. Among the joys of a joint family is the companionship that exists between relatives.

There are grandmothers who tell stories, cousins to play with, and uncles to rely on if one's father is away. There is security in crises. Parents can take vacations without worrying about with whom to leave the children. Young brides and wives are not lonely. Mothers-in-law do not generally abuse their daughters-in-law.

The flip side of the coin is that individuality disappears. A member of a joint family is a cog in a wheel, not the hub. There is also the lurking danger of

More and more girls, especially in the cities, are going to school. School curriculum is slightly different in India than in the United States. In addition to regular classes like science and literature, these girls attend yoga classes.

sexual abuse, particularly of girls. Intimidated by the perpetrator of the crime and frightened by the consequences of exposure (since the victims are often blamed), the girls, sometimes as young as 6 and 7, suffer in silence. The scars of such sordid incidents surface in later life. The joint family has almost disappeared from large cities and towns.

Adolescence

In cities, the adolescent girl goes to school. Her value in the marriage market goes up if she has a high school diploma. In traditional homes, adolescent girls are made aware of their potential as mothers-to-be. When a girl menstruates for the first time, parents call family, friends, and neighbors to celebrate the event. Special sweets made with sesame seeds and jaggery (symbols of fertility) are distributed.

This is an embarrassing celebration for the young woman, as the entire neighborhood or village gets to know that she has started menstruating. This custom, mercifully, is slowly disappearing, but is still prevalent in small towns and rural areas.

"Sitting out" is another custom that many families practice. Sitting out means that for the duration of each menstrual period, the young woman is isolated in a room. Considered unclean, she is not allowed to take part in any activity in the house. She cannot step into the kitchen or the *puja* ("poo-jah") room where prayers are conducted. She is warned not to touch plants and flowers as it is believed that these may die.

Fortunately this practice is also quickly disappearing, although much faster in the cities than in rural areas. In cities, girls go to school and take part in physical exercise and strenuous sports during those days. They are taught that menstruation is a natural process and any discomfort has simply to be borne, but can be made more comfortable with the use of sanitary napkins and specially formulated pain medication.

Since most schools are coeducational, there is every chance for a girl and boy to form a lasting friendship, which may sometimes lead to marriage. This is possible in privately run English schools, which account for less than 1% of the schools in the country. But anywhere else, it is an aberration.

From childhood, it is impressed on girls that it is wicked to have boyfriends. That is because the girl's (and hence her family's) reputation may be tarnished, and finding a marriage partner for the girl would then be difficult. So while girls may go to school along with boys, most eventually settle for an arranged marriage.

Girls are raised to believe that marriage and motherhood is the ultimate happiness. They are trained in subjects like music, embroidery, knitting, sewing, and of course, cooking, so that they can become good wives and mothers.

Celebrating Raksha Bandhan or Brothers' Day

Brothers are very protective of their sisters. If someone teases or harasses them, brothers will not stand by and watch in silence. This is true throughout the country. But in North India, there is a special day when sisters celebrate their love for their brothers.

A girl tying a *rakhee* around her brother's wrist on Raksha Bandhan.

Mohini's story

Mohini is from Rajasthan, a very backward part of the country where outdated customs still prevail. There, even if a girl who is widowed wishes to marry again, the community opposes it. Sometimes, a woman needs determination and the independence brought about by education to find happiness.

Mohini was 11 when she was married. She had completed grade 8 and therefore was literate. Her husband died even before the marriage could be consummated. Fortunately, her father encouraged her to study. But he would not think of allowing her to marry again. How could a widow marry again? No matter that she was a child widow.

Mohini studied and improved herself. She joined the Urmul Trust, a voluntary agency working in the field of health. That gave her more independence. She worked hard and made a name for herself. In villages where she worked, people began to ask for her by name.

Then she met a distant relative, a widower. They saw a mutual need for each other, she for companionship, he for companionship but also for someone to care for his young children. They decided to get married. Even the mother-in-law was happy with her son's decision and choice. Unfortunately, Mohini's brother was very ill. She thought she would wait until he recovered. He never got well and died in a few months. After observing the statutory mourning period, Mohini decided to finally marry the man of her choice. Mohini, who is now in her 30s, continues with her job and is making a new life for herself.

Opposite: The mehndi *ceremony is an essential part of the marriage festivities. All women relatives and friends have their palms decorated with henna, while the bride has the palms and backs of her hands hennaed, as well as her feet.*

That festival, Raksha Bandhan, falls in August. There is great activity before the day. Shops are full of *rakhees* ("reh-KHEYS"), amulets made of sacred silk threads adorned with silver and gold baubles. If a girl has a brother, she buys a *rakhee*. The term *brother* includes male cousins and close male friends.

On the day itself, after an early bath, the sister wears new clothes and performs *puja* or ritual worship. Then she ties the *rakhee* around her brother's wrist, puts a vermilion mark on his forehead to ward off the evil eye, and plies him with delicious sweets and other snacks.

In return, the brother promises to look after his sister—it does not matter whether she is younger or older—and gives her a gift, which could be clothes, money, or jewelry. The gift is not important. What is important is the bond of love and affection that is strengthened and kept alive.

North India celebrates Bhaiya Dooj, also to honor brothers. In Bengal, it is called Bhai Phota. Both fall in October or November, after Diwali, the Hindu Festival of Lights.

The marriage ceremony

Marriages are arranged through word of mouth, newspaper advertisements, or by introducing the couple to each other. Once the couple's horoscopes are matched, the wedding day is set. Indians have auspicious days and months for weddings. Sometimes there are so many weddings, it is referred to as "the wedding season."

Indian wedding celebrations are among the most colorful in the world, full of pomp and splendor, with festivities spread over several days.

Music and dance are an integral part of the ceremonies. In North India, *sangeet* ("sehng-geet"), or a musical evening, takes place a day or two before the actual wedding day. This happens in both the groom and the bride's house. It is an occasion for relatives and close friends to mingle. If the *sangeet* is in the groom's house, the bride's relatives are invited but the bride herself does not attend, and vice versa.

Amidst feasting, laughter, and good cheer, the women of the house sing songs meant for such occasions. They are usually funny, and on occasion ribald and emotional. For accompaniment they use a percussion instrument called a *dholki* ("DHOLE-key"). As they sing, people get up and dance a few improvised steps. Everyone applauds.

In North India, the groom comes to the bride's house riding a mare. The bride meanwhile has been dressed by friends and relatives in gorgeous clothes and jewelry. As the groom's party, the *baaraat* ("bah-raht"), approaches, there is great excitement. The bride's father and male relatives welcome the groom and his large entourage. The bride is brought face to face with her groom and there is an exchange of garlands. After

that, the *baaraat* is fed, with the bride's family waiting on them. Then the other guests are fed. Later in the evening, the marriage ceremony is performed by *pujaris* ("poo-jah-reez"), or priests, around the sacred fire.

The most important part of the marriage is the seven steps taken round the fire by the couple. After that, the groom places vermilion paste in the bride's hair parting, a symbolic gesture to show that she is now married.

In Uttar Pradesh and Punjab, the bride leaves for her husband's home immediately after the ceremony. In other places, this takes place the day after or two days later. After the ceremonies in the groom's house, most couples take a few days off to go on a honeymoon.

The Arya Samaj is a reformist movement founded on Vedic principles. During the Samaj wedding, the bride and groom are told, in simple language, what marriage is all about. Sharing everything is emphasized. The priest makes it clear that it is the duty of both to make the marriage work. After that, the priest talks to the assembled people, reminding them about their own marriage vows.

In the southern states of Tamil Nadu, Karnataka, Andhra Pradesh, and Kerala, marriages are simple affairs without the riot and color of North Indian weddings.

The wedding usually takes place in the morning or afternoon. The bride wears a white cotton *sari* dipped in turmeric. (Turmeric is believed to be auspicious.) The groom wears a *dhoti* ("DHOH-tee"), a length of cloth tied loosely round the waist. His torso is draped with a length of unstitched cloth similar to a shawl.

When the groom and his family arrive, they are received by the bride's father. In a Brahmin wedding, before the groom is let in the house, he is asked by the bride's father whether he has been to Kashi (Benares) on a pilgrimage.

When the groom says he has not, his future father-in-law hands him an umbrella and asks him to first make a pilgrimage to Kashi and then return if he wants his daughter's hand in marriage. The groom symbolically walks away with the unfurled umbrella—and returns very fast! This time he is welcomed in royal style. The bride's mother washes his feet with turmeric,

For my husband ...

Karwa Chauth ("kar-va chow-th") is one of the most important festivals in North India. It is celebrated by all married women, particularly young brides. On this day, women keep a rigorous fast—from early morning until late evening—without even a sip of water. In the evening, the women dress in bridal finery and break the fast once the moon is sighted. The fast is for the well-being of the husband. Implicit in this practice is the idea that if the husband is healthy and earns a good living, the wife too stands to gain in the eyes of society. Emancipated modern young girls are beginning to question this practice.

and she and other married women perform *arti* ("AHR-tee")—a ceremony where a tray holding a lighted lamp, *kussa* ("koos-sah") grass, vermilion paste, and turmeric is circled around the groom's head several times—to ward off the evil eye.

After the ceremonies are over, the bride changes into a shimmering silk *sari*. The groom, if he is modern, wears a three-piece Western suit. The reception for relatives and friends is held in the evening.

A Sikh wedding always takes place in a temple in the morning. It is simple and very beautiful. After the ceremony, lunch is served to those present.

Christians have church weddings as in the West. The only difference is that certain local customs are adopted, especially the tying of the *taali* ("tah-lee"), the sacred thread that married women wear, around the bride's neck.

"Five-star weddings," or weddings in posh, five-star hotels, are becoming increasingly popular. The family needs to do nothing except be present. The hotel takes care of all the arrangements, including catering.

Some young people get married in court, but by and large traditional weddings are preferred.

Among very rich people, irrespective of caste or community, weddings are usually lavish extravaganzas. There is the inevitable band playing the latest Hindi movie music.

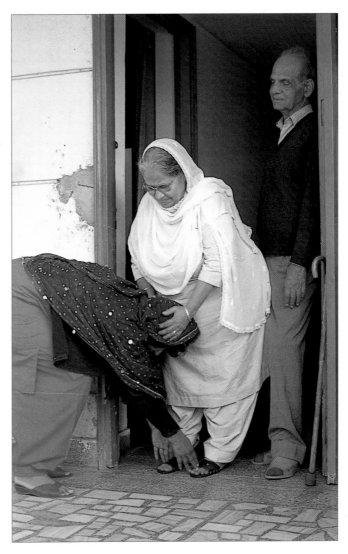

Liquor flows freely and food is overwhelmingly plentiful. The outfits people wear could keep a poor rural family of four in comfort for two months. In a relatively poor country like India, such an ostentatious display of wealth is now considered unseemly and undesirable.

A woman touches the feet of her mother-in-law as a sign of respect.

Some years ago, the government, in an attempt to curb such wasteful expenditure, imposed a limit on the number of wedding guests. But loopholes were soon found, like inviting guests at staggered times so that at any given time there were only the legal number of guests present, or having more than one function in order to include everyone.

The mother

In India, the mother has a very special place. To understand this special honor, it is important to take examine the beliefs of Hinduism. Goddesses are worshiped with at least as much fervor as gods. In the east, especially in Bengal and Orissa, the most important Hindu festival is the *Durga Puja*, dedicated to the goddess Durga. For nine whole days in October or November, all normal activity comes to a standstill. Idols of Durga are installed in different parts of the village, town, or city. On the 10th day, the idols are immersed in a pond, lake, or river. (Water figures in many Hindu rituals.)

A mother is loved and honored, and the bond between her and her children is close and strong. She will fight to protect her children, denying herself every luxury until their needs have been satisfied. Often a mother sacrifices even necessities for her children. In Indian movies, especially Hindi movies, the mother is sacrosanct. The hero loses his vocation in life if his mother is injured or dies. The mother throws herself in the path of the bullet meant for her son. Melodrama no doubt, but greatly loved by the audience.

In rural areas The mother is a harassed woman. She usually has several children to look after, including a breastfeeding baby. She has to sweep, wash the floors, cook, and fetch firewood and water from miles away. All this is time-consuming and she cannot afford the luxury of enjoying a few moments of peace and quiet with her children. As a result, the children are mostly left to their own devices. If there are girls in a family, they are expected to help with the housework.

Where there are schools, children attend classes. During those hours, the mother finishes the housework. That may also be the time she goes to fetch water, balancing at least three pots on her head and one tucked under each arm. This water has to last the family the whole day. In rural areas, water conservation has been perfected to an art because water is so precious. In the desert areas of Rajasthan, women use sand to wash the pots in which they have cooked meals. A swipe with a dry cloth and the vessels are sparkling clean—all without the use of a drop of water.

A simple rural home.

A day in a middle-class city mother's life

A.M.

5:30	Wake up
6–6:30	Fetch milk, make tea for husband
6:30	Wake children
6:40–7:20	Get children ready for school, give them breakfast, pack lunches, send them off to school
7:30–8:15	Have tea, read the paper, run the washer
8:20–8:30	Breakfast with husband, stack dishes for domestic help to wash
8:30–8:50	Shower, get ready for office
8:50–9	Leave instructions with domestic help
9	Leave for bus stop or take the car
9:30–5:30	Work

P.M.

6	Home. Make a cup of tea, relax
6:30–7	Check whether house has been cleaned up by domestic help. Attend to husband's demands
7–8	Cook while helping children with homework
8:15	Set the table, feed the children
9	Put the kids to sleep. Get their clothes, etc., ready for school the next day
9:30–10:30	Dinner with husband. Wash dishes
10:30–11:30	Relax, read, sleep

A second trip must be made for firewood. Food is cooked on a *chula* ("choo-lah"), an open stove that uses firewood for fuel. Long years of inhaling wood smoke takes a toll on the woman's health.

In areas where there are literacy classes run by nongovernmental organization, some mothers go to literacy classes with their children. Rural people are beginning to realize the importance of education.

Rajasthani women at a market.

In cities It's a different matter in cities. The population is made up of mostly middle-class people who are very ambitious for their children. A mother pushes her children hard and teaches them to be fighters in a competitive world. Mothers help with any homework the child is burdened with. Though there are hundreds of schools in a city like Delhi, the capital of India, they are insufficient to meet demand. A school like Sardar Patel Vidyalaya has 1,500 applications for the nursery class when only 25 places are available.

Increasingly, urban women are joining the workforce. They work at all kinds of jobs but prefer to take a 9-to-5 job. That gives them time to take care of routine chores like cooking and washing dishes. There is usually domestic help available, or they invest in modern appliances like a washing machine, food-processor, and vacuum cleaner. Since labor is so cheap and readily available, most people even today prefer to engage domestic help, usually a young village girl, who either lives in or comes and works part-time.

Working mothers have a tough time indeed. Indian men think it is beneath their dignity to help with the housework. Even children do not help out in

Single women—whether single by choice, widowed, divorced, or abandoned—are regarded as abnormal in India, and are viewed with suspicion, shunned, or considered loose and immoral. In certain parts of the country, even this 12-year-old child widow of an unconsummated marriage would be considered a prostitute.

urban homes. By the time they return from school and finish their homework, they are too tired to do much else. The mother does a full day's work at the office and takes charge at home.

In a tight daily schedule, mothers do not have much time for entertainment, not even for watching television. (In most homes, in any case, the television stays off because it is a distraction when the children are studying.) Despite this, if guests turn up, they are made to feel welcome. If there is harmony and happiness in a home, it is solely due to the efforts of a warm and welcoming mother.

The single woman

Since marriage is considered the most important event in a woman's life, it is thought abnormal if she is single. This includes those who are single by choice as well as those divorced, widowed, or abandoned. Whatever the cause, the stigma is pronounced. In Rajasthan, where child marriages are common, even a 12-year-old who has lost her child husband is called a prostitute.

Those who choose to be single are generally well-educated and have a job that gives them independence. Even these women are not treated equally with men, however. If they look for an apartment, landlords are suspicious, ask ridiculous questions, and lay down insulting rules. "How late at night will you come in? Will you entertain men friends? You can't have guests."

In the office it is no better. Most male colleagues feel that a woman remains single only to provide sexual interest in the office. If a woman is alone and walking home from the bus stop, she is made the butt of lewd remarks.

Women are learning to cope with being on their own. They work very hard and select their friends. They treasure their privacy and learn how to handle loneliness. The fortunate ones live in hostels for working women that are clean and comfortable, supply meals, and have facilities for washing and ironing clothes. A women's hostel is ideal for someone who wants to concentrate on work. The only disadvantage is that there is a curfew.

Rare exceptions are those single women who hold top positions in government or private companies. They have well-appointed houses, drive their own cars (or have chauffeur-driven cars), entertain, and are entertained. They are greatly respected, too, because of the high posts they occupy.

Arundhati Ghose is India's ambassador to Egypt. Before her posting, she held the post of additional secretary to the government of India and lived in one of the colonies created especially for senior government officers.

In rural areas, the condition of single women is quite tragic. It is seldom that a woman is single out of choice. She is either widowed or abandoned. Single women in villages often have a family to support. With children to look after, it is hard to make a living in places where women are not expected to work.

Old age

The government defines anyone over 60 years old as a senior citizen. According to the 1991 census, 47 million people in India are over 60, roughly 7% of the population. It is estimated that by the next century, senior citizens will make up 10% of the population.

Within the family, older people are respected and loved. Their word is law. Before any enterprise is begun, they are consulted. They are considered wise. Younger people touch their feet in reverence and invoke their blessings for prosperity or longer life.

There is no welfare system in India, so old people have to live off their savings or live with their sons. Most families like to have their parents living with them. If a couple is working, it is convenient to leave children in the care of grandparents so the children do not come back to an empty house after school. More than anything else, they need the reassurance that comes from having caring people in the house. If grandparents live on their own but close by, some parents prefer to have their children go to their grandparents' house after school and stay there until they return from work. This is what happens in most middle-class urban families.

An urban grandmother spending time with her daughter-in-law and grandchildren.

In rural areas, grandparents seldom live on their own. They have little or no savings, so they need looking after, but no one thinks of them as a burden.

Grandmother and grandfather play different roles. As the patriarch of the family, the grandfather can relax with his friends, smoke a leisurely hookah (pipe), and be served by the younger members of the family. Grandmother, on the other hand, pitches in and helps with light household chores. She chops vegetables, hangs clothes to dry, and looks after the baby, if there is one.

Children adore their grandparents. They pester them for stories, of which they seem to have an inexhaustible fund. They are pampered with the occasional gift. They love the feeling of security their grandparents give them.

Retirement homes are almost unheard of because most old people live with their children, sons in particular. One reason married couples want a son or sons is that they think sons will take care of them and make sure they are comfortable in their old age.

Not all old people have a family who will look after them. If the family is poor, then every extra mouth is a burden, and it is easiest to abandon the old. In Calcutta, hundreds of destitute men and women are picked up by the Missionaries of Charity. They are bathed, fed, and looked after. The terminally ill are put in a hospice where they can live the rest of their life with dignity.

An old tribal woman.

Other agencies help old people who have no one to care for them. Foremost among them is Help Age, a nongovernment-funded agency started in 1985 and today has a countrywide network. Help Age funds people who work at grassroots level. They aid health programs and eye and other operations. Once money is given to a grassroots agency, they monitor it very carefully and very strictly.

Women Firsts

Kiran Bedi	(b. 1949) India's first woman police officer, Kiran Bedi joined the Indian Police Service in 1977. A gutsy woman, Kiran has many laurels to her credit. She is generally considered a tough police officer and has earned the respect of her male colleagues. Presently in charge of prisons, Kiran Bedi has brought in unheard-of prison reforms.
Meera Sahib Fatima Beevi	(b. 1927) The first woman justice of the Supreme Court of India, Fatima Beevi is the second woman in the world to be appointed a supreme court justice, after Justice Sandra Day O'Connor of the U.S. Supreme Court. Fatima Beevi started her career with the Revenue Service and was also the first woman member of the Income Tax Tribunal, the highest official taxation body in India. She qualified for the judiciary in 1958. She has also served on the High Court of Kerala.
Indira Gandhi:	(1917–1984) Following in her father's (Jawaharlal Nehru, India's first prime minister) footsteps, Indira Gandhi was elected the country's first woman prime minister in 1966. She won world acclaim for her statesmanship. Within the country her slogan was *Garibi Hatao* ("geh-RI-bi heh-TAO"), which means eradicate poverty. She endeared herself to the people of India, especially to the women who voted for her in large numbers. She was also the first Indian prime minister to visit the White House. She was assassinated in 1984 by her Sikh bodyguard, in apparent retaliation for Operation Blue Star, in which she ordered the military to storm the Golden Temple in Amritsar, the Sikhs' holiest shrine, in order to put down a rebellion by Sikh separatists.Continuing the family tradition of service to India, Indira's son Rajiv succeeded her as prime minister..
Kadambini Ganguly	(1861–1913) The first Indian woman to set up practice as a doctor in India. Kadambini graduated in 1879 from Calcutta University and was awarded a gold medal. Along with Chandramukhi Basu, Kadambini became one of the country's first graduates. She then joined the Benral Medical College and graduated with a medical degree in 1886, which gave her the right to practice. She established a private practice and was a dedicated doctor, even making house calls in the dead of the night.
Geeta Ghosh	India's first woman paratrooper. She joined the Indian Air Force in 1957 and trained as a paratrooper.
Indira Hinduja	(b. 1943) The head of the Department of Gynecology and Obstetrics at KEM Hospital in Bombay. Indira made history as she was the first doctor in India to use the *in-vitro* fetilization method (popularly known as the test-tube method) to help childless couples have babies.

Anandibai Joshee	The first Indian woman to qualify as a doctor from a foreign university. In 1886, she graduated with an M.D. from the University of Philadelphia. She never set up a practice because she died of tuberculosis soon after her return to India.
Prem Mathur	(b. 1924) The first commercial woman pilot in the world, Prem Mathur got her commercial pilot's licence in 1947. In 1951, she joined Deccan Airways at Hyderabad and flew DC 3s on their scheduled flights.
Lakshmi Menon	India's first woman federal minister. In the early 1950s, Lakshmi held the important portfolio of deputy minister in the Ministry of External Affairs.
Bachendri Pal	(b. 1954) The first Indian woman to climb Mt. Everest, Bachendri Pal reached the summit on May 24, 1984. Accompanied by two male members of the expedition, Lhatoo Dorjee and Ang Dorjee, Bachendri took the familiar South Col route to reach the top of the highest peak in the work. Other women climbed to the top after Bachendri.
Muthulakshmi Reddi	(1886–1968) She was the country's first woman legislator. A dedicated nationalist social worker, educationist, and physician, she was elected to the Madras Legislative Council in 1926. She was also the first woman alderman. Together with Annie Besant, Margaret Cousins, and Sarojini Naidu, she helped set up the Indian Women's Association, which later became the All-India Women's Conference.
Vijaya Lakshmi Pandit	(1900–1990) The first woman in the world to be elected as president of the United Nations. Vijaya Lakshmi Pandit became president of the eighth General Assembly session of the United Nations in 1953. Vijaya Lakshmi was part of a family that served India—her father, Motilal Nehru, was deeply involved in India's independence movement; her brother, Jawaharlal Nehru, was India's first prime minister; and her niece, Indira Gandhi, was the country's first woman prime minister. Vijaya Lakshmi was also India's first woman ambassador when posted to Moscow from 1947 to 1949.
Cornelia Sorabjee	(1866–) The first woman lawyer in India. She went to the United Kingdom to study law and in 1923 was admitted to the Allahabad Bar (in the state of Uttar Pradesh).
Raziya Sultan	(d. 1240) First woman to rule the Delhi Sultanate from 1236 to 1240. Raziya's father, Iltutmish, appointed her to succeed him although she had brothers. She was the first Muslim woman to throw away the restricting *burqah*. Raziya insisted on being called sultan, not sultana, as sultana only meant the wife of the sultan. She was executed after an uprising by Turkish nobles on October 13, 1240.
Santosh Yadav	(b. 1964) The first woman in the world to have climbed Mt. Everest twice.

Glossary

abhinaya ("a-bhee-nah-yah") Indian art of expression without words, similar to mime.

agni pariksha ("AHG-ni peh-RIK-shah") Ordeal by fire. The woman suspected to be guilty of a crime is asked to jump into the flames. If she is not burned, she is considered pure and unsullied. The most famous instance of *agni pariksha* is in the *Ramayana*, when Rama makes Sita undergo the *agni pariksha* in order to test her chastity.

baraat ("bah-raht") The groom's entourage, usually made up of relatives and close friends who accompany him to the bride's house on the wedding day.

bhajan ("bheh-JAHNS") Devotional songs composed by *bhaktas* (adherents of the Bhakti movement) expressing an intense personal love for a particular god.

Bhakti movement A devotional movement, begun in the seventh century, emphasizing a Hindu devotee's intense emotional attachment and love for a personal god. This love is usually manifested through songs and dances.

burqah ("BUR-kah") The heavy cape, which covers a woman from head to toe, plus veil that Muslim women who observe *purdah* wear in the presence of strangers.

caste system The division of Hindus into classes based on their work.

devadasis ("they-vah-they-sees") Women dedicated to the service of god in temples. Their duty was to sing and dance in celebration of the gods.

mehar ("may-her") The dowry a Muslim man contracts to give the woman he is to marry. She may claim this at any time during the marriage, but more usually at the time of divorce.

iddat ("ID-deht") The three menstrual cycles during which a man is expected to provide maintenance to his divorced wife.

pancha satis ("pehn-chah sah-tis") The five ideal women considered models of perfection: Sita, Savitri, Draupadi, Ahalya, and Arundhati.

pativrata ("peh-ti-vrah-tah") The Indian concept of an ideal wife; one who is selflessly and steadfastly loyal to her husband.

Puranas Holy texts written by scholars between A.D. 200 and A.D. 1000.

purdah ("PERH-dah") A system of segregation where Muslim women are kept in almost complete seclusion and are not allowed any contact with men who are not close relatives.

rakhee ("reh-khee") An amulet tied by a sister to her brother's wrist during the Raksha Bandhan festival that falls in August. The colorful charm is believed to protect him from evil and bring him long life and prosperity. There is no corresponding festival for sisters.

Rig Veda The first of the holy texts, brought into India by the Aryans, on which Hindu philosophy is based. The other texts are the *Atharva Veda*, *Sama Veda*, and *Yajur Veda*.

sangeet ("sehng-geet") Literally translated, it means music. The occasion called *sangeet* is part of wedding festivities. A few days before the wedding, the bride and groom's families invite close friends and relatives and celebrate the occasion with singing and dancing. It is essentially a North Indian celebration.

saptapadi ("SEHP-tah-pah-tee") Part of the Hindu marriage ceremony in which seven steps are taken round the fire.

sati ("sah-tee") The Hindu practice of having a widow burn herself alive on her husband's funeral pyre. Although now outlawed, sati is still practiced in certain states, notably Rajasthan.

satyagraha ("SEHT-yah-grah-hah") Literally means holding fast to the truth. *Satyagraha* was Mahatma Gandhi's philosophy of nonviolent noncooperation as a means of winning independence from the British.

shunya ("shoon-yah") The concept of zero.

Sufis Followers of the Sufi religion, a mystic sect of Islam.

Further Reading

Baral, J.K. and Patnaik, K. *Gender Politics*. Discovery Publishing House, Columbia, MO, 1990.

Hawley, John S. *Sati, the Blessing and the Curse: The Burning of Wives in India*. Oxford University Press, NY, 1994.

Kumarai, Ranjana. *Brides are not for Burning: Dowry Victims in India*. Radiant Publishing, Advent, NY, 1988.

Mintum, Leigh and Kapor, Swaran. *Sita's Daughters: Coming Out of Purdah*. Oxford University Press, NY, 1993.

Mitter, Sara S. *Dharma's Daughters: Contemporary Indian Women and Hindu Culture*. Rutgers University Press, New Brunswick, NJ, 1992.

Nair, P.T. *Marriage and Dowry in India*. South Asia Boos, Columbia, MO, 1978.

Sahgal, Nayantara: *Indira Gandhi: Her Road to Power*, Frederick Ungar Publishing Co., NY, 1982.

Sources of Indian Tradition, Volumes 1 & 2. Volume 1 edited by Ainslie T. Embree, Volume 2 edited by Stephen Hay, Penguin Books, NY, 1991.

Index

Picture Credits

Susanna Burton: 21, 67, 107, 108
Joginder Chawla: 3, 5 (bottom), 9, 11,
    17, 24, 34, 40, 48, 57, 64, 65, 71, 75,
    78, 79, 80, 82, 92, 97, 111, 113, 115,
    122
Fotomedia (Sanjeev Misra): 56
Vijaya Ghose: 54
Hulton-Deutsch: 30, 83, 84, 95, 98
Richard I'Anson: 5 (top), 22, 23, 35, 76,
    103, 105, 119, 120
Sakina Kagda: 60
Bjorn Klingwall: 33, 81, 110, 116
Raghu Rai: 37
Sangeet Natak Agency: 39
Bernard Sonneville: 6, 13, 14, 29, 38, 58,
    117
Liba Taylor: 12, 26, 28, 104, 123
Matthew Titus: 7, 27, 41, 42, 45, 47, 49,
    50, 53, 55, 59, 77, 100, 101

The author thanks Abraham Thomas
and the staff at the Women's
Development Centre for their valuable
assistance.

THE ROBERT AND MEREDITH GREEN COLLECTION OF

Silver Nutmeg Graters

THE ROBERT AND MEREDITH GREEN COLLECTION OF

Silver Nutmeg Graters

John D. Davis

Introduction by Meredith W. Green

The Colonial Williamsburg Foundation

Williamsburg, Virginia

in association with

University Press of New England

HANOVER AND LONDON

I want to dedicate this book to the loving memory of my husband and fellow collector,
Dr. Robert Castleman Green, Jr.

—M. W. G.

Published in 2002 by The Colonial Williamsburg Foundation,
Williamsburg, VA 23187-1776, and University Press of New England,
Hanover, NH 03755
   www.colonialwilliamsburg.org
   www.upne.com

Photography by Hans Lorenz and Craig McDougal
Designed by Jeff Wincapaw
Produced by Marquand Books, Inc., Seattle
Color separations by iocolor, Seattle
Printed and bound in Singapore

Library of Congress Cataloging-in-Publication Data

Davis, John D., 1938–
   The Robert and Meredith Green collection of silver nutmeg graters /
John D. Davis ; introduction by Meredith W. Green.
      p. cm.
    Includes bibliographical references and index.
    ISBN 0-87935-217-5 — ISBN 1-58465-276-4
    1. Silverwork—England—Catalogs. 2. Silverwork—United
States—Catalogs. 3. Nutmeg graters—England—Catalogs.
4. Nutmeg graters—United States—Catalogs. 5. Silverwork—
Private collections—United States—Catalogs. 6. Green, Robert
Castleman—Art collections—Catalogs. 7. Green, Meredith W.—
Art collections—Catalogs. I. Title.

NK7143 .D29 2002
739.2'383—dc21

2002000847

Contents

PREFACE

Although nutmeg has been variously used for many centuries as a spice for food and drink, one does not encounter the systematic production of silver graters for this spice until the very last decades of the seventeenth century. It was at this time that a revolution in manners was beginning to take place that involved a dramatic expansion in household furnishings and personal accessories. For fashionable Britons on both sides of the Atlantic, the drinking of warm beverages (tea, coffee, and chocolate), the adopting of polite dining practices in the French mode, and the serving of punch all increasingly became highly organized social rituals. And, as these social activities became more ritualized, kits of paraphernalia used in the service and consumption of these foods and beverages appeared. Their cost depended on the ambitions and abilities of the participants to pay.

Silver nutmeg graters have been inextricably tied to the stylish service of punch since the last years of the seventeenth century. Punch became the most popular mixed alcoholic drink of the eighteenth century. Brought to England from India by sea captains and sailors, its name derives from the Hindustani word for five, the number of its basic ingredients. These included spirits, fruit juice, sugar, water, and, important here, spice, often nutmeg. Punch was drunk at home and in public, especially at taverns and coffee-houses. Principally associated with male conviviality, its drinking was seldom as sedate or mannered as the drinking of tea.

Elements of the punch equipage first appear early in the fourth quarter of the seventeenth century. One first sees punch bowls in a variety of materials and sizes, as well as that variation on the punch bowl, the monteith with its notched rim. Punch ladles, punch strainers, lemon squeezers, and leaded wineglasses also make their appearance. In fact, new modes of polite drinking and dining prompted the rapid growth of the English glass industry. From wine bottles and carboys to decanters and wineglasses, glass made for drinking purposes represents most glassware owned in Virginia in the eighteenth century.

Punch was usually made in and served from bowls. Rum and brandy were the most common spirits used. Citrus fruit yielded the preferred juice, and punch strainers are sometimes referred to in early records as lemon strainers or orange strainers. Nutmeg was most often the spice of choice, and the availability of small graters eased preparation. Iron sugar nippers or sugar hatchets cut sugar from cones into useful lumps. An available jug or bottle housed the water. Prints occasionally depict people drinking directly from the bowl and that bowls were sometimes passed from one individual to the next within a group. But in most circumstances, the wineglass was the predominant vessel used in drinking punch.

William Byrd II, who lived about thirty miles up the James River from Williamsburg, Virginia, at Westover plantation, comments on punch and its preparation in his *Natural History of Virginia*, published in 1737. "There is also made a very good, pleasant, and healthful drink, called punch," he writes, "which is produced in the following way, namely: one takes two or three bottles of water—according to whether the drink is desired strong or weak—a bottle of brandy, the juice of six or twelve lemons, which are strained through a clean cloth or a piece of linen, and a pound more or less of sugar—according to the sweetness desired.

All of this is mixed together. Finally a little nutmeg is scraped into it, after which one has a very pleasant drink."[1] One can only wonder how many times Byrd had used the grater given to him in 1719 in the preparation of punch. He had recorded in his diary on November 16th of that year, while in London, "About 8 o'clock Mrs. B-r-t-n came, who is a woman of good sense; we all ate some oysters together and Sally [Cornish] gave me a nutmeg grater to remember her by."[2]

This splendid collection, formed with great care and affection by Robert and Meredith Green, systematically represents English and American nutmeg graters in all their breadth and detail. The following catalog is structured on the chronological sequence of fashionable types with London silversmiths playing a major role from the late seventeenth century onward in the production of silver nutmeg graters. Birmingham entrepreneurs of the late eighteenth and nineteenth centuries made important and distinctive contributions. Handsome graters of melon form by Gorham & Co. and Tiffany & Co. from the turn of the last century and an evocative copy of an early heart-shaped one by William de Matteo, former master silversmith of Colonial Williamsburg, complete this amazing collection. There are so many wonderful objects that relate to one another or provide solitary revelations and pleasure. This collection will always be an occasion for the remembrance of Robert and Meredith Green.

1. Richmond Croom Beatty and William J. Mulloy, eds., *William Byrd's Natural History of Virginia; or the Newly Discovered Eden* (Richmond, Va., 1940), p. 92.

2. William Byrd, *The London Diary, 1717–1721, and Other Writings*, ed. Louis B. Wright and Marion Tinling (New York, N.Y., 1958), p. 341.

Meredith W. Green

INTRODUCTION
THE NUTMEG ODYSSEY

When this collection was exhibited for the first time, the question immediately asked was: "How did a small-town physician in the Blue Ridge Mountains of Virginia become a collector of English silver nutmeg graters?" The answer is long and circuitous. My husband, Dr. Robert Green, Jr., having just completed his years of advanced training at the Mayo Clinic, went back with me to my home in rural Southside Virginia, to help me sort through some of my late father's business affairs. One Sunday morning, my husband was called to the local hospital to see a woman who seemed to be dying from the ingestion of a can of nutmeg spice. He discovered that this married woman, with several children, had heard that nutmeg could serve as an abortion agent. Her heart was racing, her face was flushed, she showed rapid breathing, and she was nauseated. Dr. Green called the company that manufactured the nutmeg spice and, while they had little to offer in the way of help for the unfortunate lady, they did encourage Dr. Green to carry out any procedures that might be useful, saying they would gladly underwrite the cost.

The patient recovered, yet my husband remained interested in the case and continued to research the medical literature. He found that there had not been a case of nutmeg poisoning reported in the previous twenty-five years. He also read about men in prison using nutmeg to make a drink on which they could get high. As he continued his investigation, Dr. Green decided to write about this case for publication in *The Journal of the American Medical Association*. The article is reprinted in the appendix.

At the time of the publication of his article, we were moving to Winchester, Virginia, where my husband was born and wanted to return to practice medicine.

This was in July 1958. Upon arrival in Winchester, he received a call from the editors at *Time* magazine expressing interest in his nutmeg article, and stating that they were sending a photographer and a reporter. The editors indicated that they would feature his article in the medical section of the following week's issue.

Did Ever Pride Go Before a Fall? Here my husband was arriving in his hometown to start his career, and he was going to be written about in *Time*. What wonderful publicity! Then came a second call. Another story had wider appeal, so the editors were junking the whole nutmeg article idea!

Many months later, I took a visiting friend to see Harpers Ferry, made famous by John Brown's raid. We happened to wander into an antique shop. There, we spotted a small, round silver item that looked somewhat like a seed with a wrinkled skin. Opening it, we found a piece of a nutmeg. The shopkeeper said she had been told that this object was a nutmeg grater (no. 58). Remembering the disappointment over the *Time* article, the grater was purchased for Dr. Green's birthday and also to celebrate the publication of the article in the esteemed medical journal in 1959.

As it turned out, my husband loved the little silver nutmeg grater, had a stand made for it, and prominently displayed it on his desk under a glass dome of the type often used to display watches. Then a few months later, when my friend and I were in London, we went to the London Silver Vaults and there discovered tubelike, lipstick-size silver items. We were told that these were very early nutmeg graters. So early, in fact, that they did not have any of the valued hallmarks. Two of these pierced-open graters were acquired as trip gifts for Dr. Green (nos. 5 and 7).

And with three graters thereby begins the collection! This hobby was to last over the next forty years and involve many trips to London and other places in England, as well as shops and sales in this country. It became the focus of many of our trips, a sort of guiding factor, and gave us much delight when a new and unusual grater was discovered.

In fact, in the early 1960s when we were in London, we discovered an antiques store specializing in silver and jewelry on Bond Street called S. J. Phillips, Ltd. An elderly gentleman, almost a stereotypical Englishman, waited on us and was fascinated when he found out that we were interested in collecting nutmeg graters. He had a small collection, and in great detail he told us about the hallmarks, some of the history of the makers, and the dates. This was a real education.

While we stood there that rainy March morning a woman charged in (she had to be at least a duchess), and asked if her tiara was ready. This was quickly produced for her by one of the other salesmen, she tried it on, gave it back to the man, and sailed out of the store, while her driver-valet waited for it to be boxed. This was pretty impressive to us, for we were shopping in a place where royalty also did business.

Our gentle salesman told us the price of each nutmeg grater: something like £120, £115, £75, £100, and £135. No grater had a price tag. They were laid out on black velvet. From memory, the cost of each had been given. Tentatively, and using his American antique dealing technique, Dr. Green asked what would be the cost if he bought all of them. This led to our dear man disappearing behind the gate that divided the front of the establishment and what seemed to be an office area. We could see him in earnest conversation with a man seated at a big desk. Then he returned and quietly told us that we could have all five of them for £500. We pointed out that one was priced below £100 and therefore we wanted to offer £475 for the group. Again he left, and, after a short consultation, he returned to say the offer was accepted.

Thus we were introduced to "dealing" in impressive places. For sometimes a guard stood at the door letting in a customer only after careful scrutiny, and we had learned to bargain, to make an offer, to walk away, and to come back with a new offer, even in awesome surroundings.

One of our most fascinating encounters occurred in the mid-1970s when we arrived later in March than our usual trip time. Our first stop was to see our man at Phillips who, for the staid Englishman he was, practically hugged us. He said he was so afraid we were not coming and the wealthy oil Arabs were buying up everything. He said he had on hand the most perfect item for us—a gold nutmeg grater. We were astounded. We had never heard of one being made in gold and thought it was too soft a metal for such use. We asked whether we could take the grater down the street to Sotheby's and discuss its authenticity with the head of the silver sales department, a man we had already dealt with several times. This we were allowed to do, and there were told that it was indeed a rare piece, made by A. J. Strachan, one of London's most distinguished goldsmiths. Once back at Phillips, we found that the price of this gold grater exceeded the limit of our American Express® card, which meant that we had to add a check to acquire this precious grater!

The only other time we found a group of graters on sale together happened in the mid-1980s when we were returning from a trip to Egypt and stopped in London on the way home. There was a wonderful store called Tessiers, Ltd., from which we had bought some graters. At this time, they had obtained a small collection of about three dozen graters and printed an attractive brochure about them. It was again a cold and rainy day in late March, and Dr. Green was sick with something like flu that he had acquired along the way. While sweating from a temperature, nauseated, and wrapped up in his wet raincoat, he sat at the counter examining each grater. By this time, we had a small collection and some of these boxes that were for sale were mundane, run-of-the-mill graters, while some were the work of more outstanding silversmiths and therefore should be acquired even if similar to ones we already had. There were some graters that were unique—not in our collection and we were thrilled to have a chance to purchase them. So, with sheer, grim determination, the examination of each progressed and twelve new graters were bought.

One of the delightful aspects of this collecting activity was the acquaintances we made. A woman in our community who had come from Scotland loved antiques, and by mail she introduced Dr. Green to Mr. Bell of Aberdeen, Scotland. This led to a long and active correspondence and to the acquisition over the years of at least a half-dozen graters.

At Asprey's we had met another charming Englishman, Alastair Dickenson, who later left that company and founded his own. Through the years while he was with Asprey's and in the years that followed when he was independent, he was wonderful about sending us pictures of unusual graters and offering us the opportunity to buy them.

And at antique shows in Washington and New York, we encountered a delightful man, Sandy Stearns of The Hobart House. We were often in London at the time of The Chelsea Antiques Fair and Sandy would be there. One memorable afternoon, we were the guests of Sandy and his wife for the fabulous seven-course tea at The Ritz, London. Later, Sandy visited us both in Virginia and at our Massachusetts summer place.

Between "hunting" trips for graters, Dr. Green began to read about them. One of the first books he found, and really one of the best ever written, was Elizabeth B. Miles's 1966 book, *The English Silver Pocket Nutmeg Grater*. At the beginning of her book, Mrs. Miles describes how, in the reign of Elizabeth I, after the establishment of the East India Trading Company, spices of all kinds were imported into England. First used by royalty, spices were soon aggressively consumed by the general public, who used them for medicinal purposes, as fumigants, and to add exotic flavors to their food and drinks.

She writes that when the use of silver utensils became prevalent and showy in the seventeenth century, their presence apparently resulted in many robberies and murders in public houses and taverns. This led to the enactment of a law in about 1695 that forbade the inn- and tavern keepers from displaying any silver utensils except spoons. Consequently, those wealthy people who preferred silver to wooden implements resorted to carrying their personal silver eating utensils in traveling cases. These cases usually consisted of a large tumbler cup with a knife, fork, and spoon fitted in, sometimes containers for salt and pepper, and a nutmeg grater. Frequently, the nutmeg grater was of an acorn shape with a stem in which there was a corkscrew. (Mrs. Miles points out that this combination of grater and corkscrew created a shape that was described as macelike because of its resemblance to the ornamental staff carried by the lord mayor and other dignitaries. She also wrote that the mace could have been a pun based on the fact that the outside shell of a nutmeg is called mace.) So, the lucky owner of the mace-shaped grater was prepared to open his bottle of wine, and then grate the nutmeg into his drink. These traveling utensils were usually in a shagreen, or leather, case. (There are three of these traveling cases in this collection, nos. 34–36.)

Following this history of the introduction of spices into England and the use of silver eating utensils, Mrs. Miles gives an excellent history of the hallmarking of English silver. She points out that from 1697 to 1720, the leopard's head (indicating a London-made object) became the lion's head and the figure of a woman, Britannia, plus the first two letters of the maker's surname, were used to indicate that the metal was of much higher standard than mere sterling. After 1720, the sterling standard was reinstated and remains to the present. But from 1784 to 1890, a fifth mark, a sovereign's head, was used to indicate that the duty had been paid. However, small objects such as nutmeg graters were exempted from duty and frequently have no marks, or only maker's marks. Silver objects made in Birmingham from 1773 had an anchor to represent the city. The other marks were a lion passant (signifying the proper amount of silver), a letter for the date (which changed every May), and the maker's marks (usually initials). For graters from London and Birmingham, the five hallmarks were not always all present. Sometimes the marks would be on the lid and at other times inside the graters.

Dr. Green's notes indicate that the small nutmeg graters did not become prevalent until the introduction of pockets in men's pants around the last quarter of the seventeenth century. Some graters were made of ivory, bone, and hardwood, but the more well-to-do preferred silver. Also, the high cost of nutmeg restricted its use, and so nutmeg graters did not become prevalent until the late eighteenth century.

Also, in his notes, Dr. Green points out that the rasping surface of the grater consisted of tiny holes punched in the hammered silver. By 1790, rolled steel, which had been treated to have a hard blue film, was used and continues to be visible in the graters.

The earlier graters were plain, often either heart shaped or cylindrical. The engraving frequently consisted of lines or a simple drawn flower, one somewhat like a tulip but often called a rose. No. 9 in this collection is an example of the cylinder-type grater made with pierced steel. The heart-shaped grater, no. 14, is not hallmarked and this seems to have been true of many small objects. In this case, the grater is fixed to the body of the box, with the top and bottom covers hinged in order that the grated nutmeg could pass through it.

By the eighteenth century, the shape of graters changed. No. 78 is typical of those with a hinged lid and removable grater, which allowed the nutmeg to be stored inside. At century's end, silversmiths became much more creative and graters were made in the shape of barrels, maces, and urns.

In the late eighteenth century and the beginning of the nineteenth century, as the middle class became wealthier and could afford both items of silver and nutmeg itself, graters became much more common and were made in many different shapes such as eggs, fruits, and walnuts. But it is interesting to note that the shape of the nutmeg was rarely used. The boxes became much more elaborately decorated with bright-cut engraving, reeding, engine turning, some leaf designs, and an occasional coat of arms. However, it has been pointed out that although many graters have initials or monograms, few are found with crests, suggesting that those who could afford more expensive wines did not need to conceal the bad taste with the nutmeg's aromatic flavor. Initially, the graters were made primarily by silversmiths of London such as T. Phipps and E. Robinson, S. Barker, and J. Robins. But as the existence of graters became more popular, many were made by numerous other artisans and by the silversmiths of Birmingham, including S. Pemberton, J. Willmore, and J. Taylor, to name a few of the well-known and quite prolific producers.

Much of this history of English silver nutmeg graters has come from notes that Dr. Green made, for he had always wanted to do a small book about these lovely graters and the fun we had collecting them. Fortunately, for those who like to collect beautiful small objects, the talented English silversmiths of the seventeenth and eighteenth centuries provided a great many wonderful possibilities. And acquiring this collection of graters added a great deal of pleasure to both our trips and our lives. I must express great appreciation to John Davis, senior curator of metals at the Colonial Williamsburg Foundation, for this book never would have been published without his help and persistent encouragement.

Catalog

LUTE

1670–1690

*Because of its early date, unusually large size,
and uncommon design, this grater stands by itself
rather than with a later group of singular examples,
although this grater certainly qualifies as one.*

1. **Unmarked**

   Silver with infills of pigmented resin
   England or Holland, ca. 1680
   OL. 4¾"
   L1999-104

   This extraordinary example has
   a sliding rectangular panel in the
   engraved face of the body that
   conceals the grater.

SILVER-MOUNTED COWRIE SHELLS

1680–1720

Mounted shells, in particular cowries, served not only as nutmeg graters in the late seventeenth and early eighteenth centuries, but also as snuff and tobacco boxes.

2. Unmarked

Probably London, England, ca. 1690
OL. 3⅜"
L1999-95

3. Unmarked

Probably London, England, ca. 1690
Later cipher *RCT* engraved on shield
at intersection of mounts
OL. (with ring) 4¼"
L1999-106

4. Unmarked

England, ca. 1710
Unidentified crest with ornamented
initials *JR* engraved on face of cover
OL. 3⁵⁄₁₆", OW. 2³⁄₁₆"
L1999-91

Early Cylinders

1680–1710

This common early type is usually simply made from seamed silver tubes with a pull-off cap at one end. They are usually embellished with somewhat crude geometric or floral engraving. Early cylinders pierced with geometric shapes are relatively rare. The graters themselves are of seamed tubular form, usually with one end closed. They fit loosely within the cylindrical case.

Left to right; front

5. Unmarked

Probably London, England, ca. 1690
OL. $2^{5}/_{16}$", DIAM. $^{13}/_{16}$"
L1999-181

6. TH conjoined (unidentified)

Probably London, England, ca. 1685
Owner's initials *ES* engraved on end of case
L. (case) $2^{3}/_{8}$", DIAM. (case) $^{13}/_{16}$";
L. (grater) $2^{3}/_{16}$"
L1999-137

7. BC/99 (unidentified)

Probably London, England, ca. 1700
L. (case) $2^{3}/_{4}$", DIAM. (case) $^{13}/_{16}$";
L. (grater) $2^{1}/_{4}$"
L1999-136

8. I·H (unidentified)

Probably London, England, ca. 1690
Owner's initials *ML* engraved on end of case
L. (case) $2^{7}/_{8}$", DIAM. (case) $^{13}/_{16}$";
L. (grater) $2^{7}/_{16}$"
L1999-203

9. Thomas Kedden

London, England, ca. 1695
L. (case) $2^{13}/_{16}$", DIAM. (case) $^{15}/_{16}$";
L. (grater) $1^{13}/_{16}$"
L1999-205

Thomas Kedden, the maker of this grater and nos. 10 and 15, is the most frequently encountered producer of early nutmeg graters.

10. Thomas Kedden

London, England, ca. 1705
Owner's initials *MP* engraved on face of case
L. (case) $2^{3}/_{4}$", DIAM. (case) $^{15}/_{16}$";
L. (grater) $1^{13}/_{16}$"
L1999-204

HEARTS

1690–1790

Heart-shaped examples are fitted with upper and lower hinged covers to ease removal of the ground nutmeg that had passed through the grater. Early examples tend to be engraved in a manner similar to the cases of early cylinders.

Center: clockwise from top

11. Unmarked
Probably London, England, ca. 1685
OH. 1½", OL. 2⅜", OW. 1⅞"
L1999-103

12. Unmarked
England, ca. 1720
OH. 1½", OL. 2¾", OW. 2"
L1999-146

13. Joseph Richardson II and Nathaniel Richardson
Philadelphia, Pennsylvania, ca. 1785
Owner's initials *D·M* engraved on face of body between hinges
OH. 1³⁄₁₆", OL. 1⅞", OW. 1⁷⁄₁₆"
L1999-87

American nutmeg graters are uncommon. This example, marked by the fashionable Philadelphia partnership of Joseph Richardson II and Nathaniel Richardson, shows the extended popularity of this shape. The inventory of their shop, taken May 5, 1790, lists "5 Pocket Nutmeg graters."

14. Unmarked
Probably London, England, ca. 1720
Owner's cipher *EF* doubled and reversed engraved on face of upper cover
OH. 1⅛", OL. 1⁵⁄₁₆", OW. 1⅛"
L1999-135

15. Thomas Kedden
London, England, ca. 1695
Owners' initials *H/I❋S* engraved on face of upper cover
OH. 1", OL. 1⅝", OW. 1⅛"
L1999-209

16. Unmarked
Probably London, England, ca. 1690
Owner's initials *WF* inexpertly engraved on face of lower cover
OH. ⅞", OL. 1½", OW. 1⅛"
L1999-155

17. TH conjoined (unidentified)
London, England, ca. 1685
OH. 1¹⁄₁₆", OL. 1¹¹⁄₁₆", OW. 1⁷⁄₁₆"
L1999-179

Rococo Urns and an Egg

1745–1760

The inverted pear-shaped bodies of the urns and the scrolled and naturalistic chased decoration are expressive elements of the rococo taste.

18. Possibly Samuel Meriton I

London, England, ca. 1750
Wooden case covered in shagreen
and lined with red velvet
H. (case) 1^{15}/$_{16}$"; H. (grater) 1^{3}/$_{4}$",
DIAM. (grater base) ^{5}/$_{8}$"
L1999-177

19. Maker unidentified

London, England, ca. 1750
OH. 1^{13}/$_{16}$", DIAM. (base) ^{11}/$_{16}$"
L1999-192

20. Probably David Field

London, England, ca. 1750
Owner's initials *MS* in script
engraved on underside of base
OH. 2^{3}/$_{16}$", DIAM. (base) ^{3}/$_{4}$"
L1999-191

This maker specialized in the production of small work, especially acorn-shaped nutmeg graters with corkscrews (nos. 22 and 24).

21. Possibly Samuel Meriton I

London, England, ca. 1760
OL. 1^{9}/$_{16}$"
L1999-174

Acorns

1740–1830

Nutmeg graters of acorn form were especially popular during the third quarter of the eighteenth century. Those fitted with a corkscrew are often found in travel canteens of the period, and they often bear the mark associated with David Field.

22. Probably David Field

London, England, ca. 1750
Owners' initials *AL/❋* engraved on end of corkscrew cover
OL. 4"
L1999-90

23. Probably David Field

London, England, ca. 1760
OL. 3¼"
L1999-110

24. Probably David Field

London, England, ca. 1760
Owner's initials *BT* in script later engraved on face of body
OL. 3¼"
L1999-206

The inclusion of an iron or steel punch, rather than the customary corkscrew, is unusual. The punch appears to be original.

25. W&E (unidentified)

England, ca. 1820
Wooden case covered in shagreen and lined with red velvet
H. (case) 2⁹/₁₆"; L. (grater) 2⅛"
L1999-148

26. Unmarked

Probably London, England, ca. 1755
OL. 2"
L1999-126

Barrels

1785–1845

Nutmeg graters of this type are reminiscent of and may derive from fitted pairs of beakers of barrel form that pull apart in the middle in the same manner. This form is also popular for graters with bodies of turned wood or nut.

Left; back row; front row

27. Samuel Kirk

Baltimore, Maryland, ca. 1840
Owner's initials *SM* in ornamented
script engraved on end
OH. 2⅝"
L1999-100

American nutmeg graters are
uncommon. This example is
quite large, regardless of origin.

28. Samuel Meriton II

London, England, ca. 1790
OH. 15/16"
L1999-171

29. Peter and Anne Bateman

London, England, 1793/4
OH. 1 9/16"
L1999-93

30. Thomas Meriton

London, England, 1800/1
OH. 1 15/16"
L1999-180

31. Unmarked

Gold
England, ca. 1800
OH. 1¼"
L1999-86

Solid gold nutmeg graters are
extremely rare (*see also* no. 77).

32. IS (unidentified)

London, England, 1796/7
OH. 1 5/16"
L1999-168

33. William Bateman I

London, England, 1819/20
OH. 1 15/16"
L1999-130

Canteens

1792–1814

Canteens such as these with a large beaker, generally of oval plan, fitted with a drop-in plug for flatware and other accessories, and contained within a leather-covered case, were intended for travelers. A nutmeg grater was often among the useful accessories included.

34. Samuel Meriton II and various makers

London, England, 1792/3
Engraved with the cipher *CR* with royal crown above
L. (grater) 1 $^{11}/_{16}$"
L1999-85

This canteen is believed to have been owned by Queen Charlotte (1744–1818), wife of King George III. The outer case is missing.

35. Probably William Parker

Probably assembled and retailed by
William Eley I and William Fearn
London, England, 1803/4
Wooden case covered in red, scythed
leather and lined with blue silk
L. (grater) $5^{5/16}$"
L1999-83

36. Thomas Phipps, Edward
    Robinson II, and James
    Phipps II

Silver gilt
London, England, 1813/4
Engraved owner's cipher *RT* with
Gustaf./1820. also engraved on face
of beaker
Wooden case covered in red, scythed
leather and lined with blue velvet
L. (grater) 5³⁄₈"
L1999-84

This firm made all the pieces, except
for bladed flatware, including the
nutmeg grater of urn type with
corkscrew.

Neoclassic Urns
1788–1830

These all work in the same way. When the hinged cover is raised, the body, which is divided in half vertically and hinged across the base, opens to reveal the grater.

37. Robert Barker

London, England, 1794/5
GINGER engraved on face of cover; unidentified crest engraved on face of body
OH. 2⅝"
L1999-105

The inscription *GINGER* is a useful reminder that these graters were sometimes used for spices other than nutmeg.

38. Thomas Phipps and Edward Robinson II

London, England, 1788/9
OH. 2⅝"
L1999-145

39. Unmarked

Probably China, ca. 1820
Owner's initial *C* engraved on face of body
OH. 2¹⁵⁄₁₆"
L1999-101

40. Cu (unidentified)

Europe, ca. 1830
Owners' initials *AHG* in script engraved on face of body
OH. 3⁵⁄₁₆"
L1999-113

41. Unmarked

Possibly Holland, ca. 1800
OH. 3"
L1999-97

KITCHEN NUTMEG GRATERS

1802–1821

This type obviously imitates, on a greatly reduced scale, various patterns of base-metal graters made for kitchen use.

42. **Thomas Phipps and James Phipps II**

London, England, 1819/20
Unidentified owner's crest engraved on face of hinged base cover
OH. 4⁹/₁₆", DIAM. (base) 2"
L1999-111

43. **Joseph Ash I**

London, England, 1803/4
Owner's initial *T* in script engraved on face of base
OH. 4⁵/₁₆", OL. 1⅛", OW. 1¹⁵/₁₆"
L1999-112

44. **Thomas Phipps and Edward Robinson II**

London, England, 1802/3
OH. 4⁵/₁₆", OL. 1⅛", OW. 2¼"
L1999-211

45. **Probably James Ruell**

London, England, 1816/7
Owner's crest and cipher *CAS* engraved within a bright-cut reserve on face of back
OH. 3⅝", OL. ¹⁵/₁₆", OW. 1¾"
L1999-210

46. **George Pearson**

London, England, 1820/1
OH. 4³/₁₆", OL. 1⅛", OW. 1⅞"
L1999-125

LATE CYLINDERS
1784–1831

*Unlike early cylinders (nos. 5–10), these are
constructed in much the same way as neoclassic
urns (nos. 37–41). The flat covers of the sterling
examples are hinged, as are the front panels of the
bodies, with the graters fixed behind. Fused-plated
examples usually avoid problematic hinges and
have simple pull-off covers and tubular bodies.*

47. Hester Bateman
London, England, 1784/5
OL. 2^{15}/$_{16}$"
L1999-138

48. Probably James Ruell
London, England, 1795/6
Unidentified owner's crest engraved
on face of cover
OL. 2^{3}/$_{8}$"
L1999-208

49. Maker's mark indistinct
England, ca. 1825
Owner's crest and motto of Saint Clair
engraved on face of cover
OL. 2^{1}/$_{4}$"
L1999-147

50. Charles Rawlings and William Summers
London, England, 1830/1
Owner's initials *LC* in script
engraved on face of cover
OL. 2^{1}/$_{2}$"
L1999-197

51. Unmarked
Fused silver plate (Sheffield plate)
Sheffield or Birmingham, England,
ca. 1800
OL. 2^{7}/$_{8}$"
L1999-99

52. Unmarked
Fused silver plate (Sheffield plate)
Sheffield or Birmingham, England,
ca. 1800
OL. 3^{1}/$_{16}$"
L1999-178

TABLE GRATERS
1813–1845

These examples are of generous size and of individual design, and they do not share with most of the others the property of personal portability.

53. **Maker's mark indistinct**
London, England, 1815/6
Owner's initials *AS* in script
engraved on face of body
OH. 1⅝", OW. (with handle) 3⁷⁄₁₆",
DIAM. (base) 1⁷⁄₁₆"
L1999-117

54. **Thomas Phipps,
Edward Robinson II, and
James Phipps II**
London, England, 1813/4
OH. 2¼", DIAM. 2⁹⁄₁₆"
L1999-119

55. **Unmarked**
Probably India, ca. 1840
Unidentified owner's crest engraved
on face of cover
OH. 2⅜", DIAM. (cover) 2½",
DIAM. (base) 2¹⁄₁₆"
L1999-98

Natural Shapes
1851–1907

*Naturalistic forms, such as melons, beehives,
gourds, and even nutmegs, represent the most
popular choices for nutmeg graters of the Victorian
period in England and America.*

56. Abraham Brownett
Silver gilt
London, England, 1864/5
Owner's monogram *MP* in relief
applied to cover
OH. 1⁹⁄₁₆", OL. 1³⁄₄"
L1999-115

57. Unidentified manufacturer
Electroplate
Probably England, ca. 1860
Pattern number *7253* and probable
workman's mark *C* stamped on
bottom; owner's initial *H* in script
engraved on underside
OH. 1¹⁵⁄₁₆", DIAM. (base) 1⁷⁄₁₆"
L1999-139

58. Thomas Hilliard and
Edward Thomason
Birmingham, England, 1853/4
OH. 1¹⁄₄", OL. 1⁹⁄₁₆"
L1999-202

59. Thomas Hilliard and
Edward Thomason
Birmingham, England, 1861/2
Owners' initials *MFW* in script
engraved on shield applied to body
above clasp
OH. 1¹⁄₄", OL. 1¹¹⁄₁₆"
L1999-142

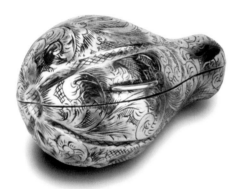

60. **Thomas Hilliard and Edward Thomason**

Birmingham, England, 1856/7
OL. 2"
L1999-160

61. **Thomas Hilliard and Edward Thomason**

Birmingham, England, 1853/4
Owners' initials *JAT* in script
engraved on face of cover
OH. 1³⁄₁₆", OL. 1⁵⁄₈"
L1999-163

62. **Thomas Hilliard and**
   Edward Thomason

   Birmingham, England, 1851/2
   OH. 1³/₁₆", OL. 1¹/₂"
   L1999-108

63. **Thomas Hilliard and**
   Edward Thomason

   Birmingham, England, ca. 1885
   OH. 1³/₁₆", OL. 1¹/₂"
   L1999-154

64. **Gorham & Co.**
   Providence, Rhode Island, 1886
   OH. 1½", OL. 2"
   L1999-131

65. **Gorham & Co.**
   Providence, Rhode Island, 1890
   OH. 1½", OL. 2"
   L1999-156

66. **Gorham & Co.**
   Providence, Rhode Island, ca. 1895
   Owner's initial *W* in script engraved
   on face of body
   OH. 1⁹/₁₆", OL. 2¹/₁₆"
   L1999-141

67. **Retailed and possibly made
   by William H. Saxton, Jr.**
   New London, Connecticut, ca. 1885
   OH. 1⁷/₁₆", OL. 2¼"
   L1999-159

68. **Tiffany & Co.**
   New York, New York, ca. 1905
   OH. 1³/₈", OL. 1⁹/₁₆"
   L1999-161

69. **Tiffany & Co.**
   Gilt lined
   New York, New York, ca. 1890
   OH. 1⁵/₈", OL. 1¹³/₁₆"
   L1999-157

Boats

1823–1920

Although the first two of these examples could have been used to grate nutmeg and other spices, they were probably intended as snuff or tobacco rasps.

70. **Probably Charles Rawlings**
London, England, 1823/4
Owners' initials *AJM* engraved in
script on face of cover
OH. 1^{11}/$_{16}$", OL. (with ring) 7^{11}/$_{16}$",
OW. 1^{15}/$_{16}$"
L1999-122

71. **Pittar & Co.**
Calcutta, India, ca. 1840
OH. 2^{1}/$_{8}$", OL. (with ring) 7^{1}/$_{16}$",
OW. 1^{7}/$_{8}$"
L1999-96

72. **Dominick & Haff**
Newark, New Jersey, and New York,
New York, ca. 1910
Owners' initials *LBF* in script
engraved on face of cover
OH. 1^{5}/$_{16}$", OL. (with ring) 4^{1}/$_{8}$",
OW. 1^{1}/$_{2}$"
L1999-144

SINGULAR EXAMPLES

1793–1812

*Some nutmeg graters are of truly exceptional merit,
such as the exquisite memorial example (no. 73),
the gilt pair (nos. 74 and 75), the large engraved
one (no. 76), and the unfolding gold example with
its tailored appearance (no. 77). Each of these is
also in splendid condition.*

73. **Probably John Robins**
Silver gilt
London, England, 1793
Inscribed *Mrs Eliz: Hodgson · died ·
16 · sep: 1793 · aged · 66* with owners'
initials *LB* and *A · M* engraved on
upper face of body concealed by
rim of cover when closed
Wooden case covered in red leather
and lined with cream silk and blue
velvet
L. (case) 2³⁄₈"; H. (grater) 1¹⁄₈",
L. (grater) 1¹⁵⁄₁₆", W. (grater) 1¹⁄₄"
L1999-114

The memorial inscription to
Mrs. Hodgson is in gold on black
enamel while the owner's initials
are in script in gold applied against
a ground of braided hair under glass
on the underside of the cover.

74. and 75. Thomas Phipps and Edward Robinson II

Silver gilt
London, England, 1795/6
Owner's initials *EG* in script engraved on face of one cover (no. 74),
and *AS* in script engraved on the face
of the other (no. 75)
Wooden cases covered in scythed,
red leather and lined with cream
and green silks and green woolen
broadcloth
L. (cases) 2¼"; H. (graters) ¹³/₁₆",
L. (graters) 1¹⁵/₁₆", W. (graters) 1⁵/₁₆"
L1999-151-152

EG was for Emma Garrick, the first
wife of David Garrick, nephew and
godson of the famous actor of the
same name. *AS* stood for Arabella
Shaw, sister of David Garrick, nephew
and godson of the actor. The death of
Garrick in 1795 may have occasioned
the production of this pair of graters.

76. George Smith II and
Thomas Hayter

London, England, 1804/5
Unidentified crest engraved on face
of cover
OH. 1⅛", OL. 3¼", OW. 2¹⁄₁₆"
L1999-124

77. **Alexander James Strachan**
Gold
London, England, 1811/2
Owner's initials *MM* in script with an
earl's coronet above in relief on cover
OH. 1⁷⁄₁₆"
L1999-89

This maker is particularly noted for
his production of splendid gold boxes.
He was the principal supplier to the
royal goldsmiths Rundell, Bridge,
and Rundell, who, in turn, made them
available to the Crown for presentation
purposes. His work is of the utmost
technical refinement, as in this fas-
tidious nutmeg grater with its con-
trasting shades of gold and tailored
decoration for its noble owner.

LONDON

1745–1813

This section highlights representative London work of the late eighteenth and early nineteenth centuries by prominent producers of nutmeg graters such as Hester Bateman, Susanna Barker, and the partnership of Thomas Phipps and Edward Robinson II.

78. **Unmarked**
Probably London, England, ca. 1750
Unidentified owner's crest engraved on face of cover
OH. 1³/₁₆", OL. 2³/₁₆", OW. 2¹/₁₆"
L1999-107

79. **Robert Hennell I**
London, England, ca. 1790
Indistinct owner's initials engraved on face of cover
OH. 1¹/₁₆", OL. 1⁵/₈", OW. 1⁷/₁₆"
L1999-199

80. **Unmarked**
Probably London, England, ca. 1790
Unidentified family crest with earl's coronet above engraved on face of body
OH. 1⁷/₁₆"
L1999-140

81. Thomas Phipps and
    Edward Robinson II

London, England, 1788/9
Owner's initials *HW* in script
engraved on face of cover
OH. 1$^{1}/_{16}$", OL. 2$^{1}/_{8}$", OW. 1$^{5}/_{16}$"
L1999-190

82. Thomas Phipps and
    Edward Robinson II

London, England, 1790/1
OH. $^{15}/_{16}$", OL. 1$^{7}/_{8}$", OW. 1$^{5}/_{16}$"
L1999-167

83. Thomas Phipps and
    Edward Robinson II

London, England, 1790/1
OH. 1", OL. 1$^{7}/_{8}$", OW. 1$^{5}/_{16}$"
L1999-189

84. Thomas Phipps and
    Edward Robinson II

London, England, 1804/5
OH. 1$^{1}/_{8}$", OL. 2$^{7}/_{16}$", OW. 1$^{11}/_{16}$"
L1999-118

85. Thomas Phipps and
    Edward Robinson II

London, England, 1799/1800
OH. $^{15}/_{16}$", OL. 3$^{1}/_{8}$", OW. 2$^{3}/_{16}$"
L1999-132

Top to bottom

86. John Hutson

London, England, 1795/6
Owner's initials *AJ* in script engraved
on face of cover; arms of Landon
impaling Palmer engraved
on underside of base
OH. $^{15}/_{16}$", OL. $2^{1}/_{16}$", OW. $1^{1}/_{4}$"
L1999-143

87. Hester Bateman

London, England, 1786/7
OH. $1^{1}/_{8}$", OL. $1^{13}/_{16}$", OW. $1^{1}/_{8}$"
L1999-207

88. Peter Carter

London, England, 1787/8
Owner's initials *MF* in script engraved
on face of cover
OH. $2^{3}/_{16}$", OL. $2^{1}/_{16}$", OW. $1^{5}/_{16}$"
L1999-162

89. Probably Solomon Hougham

London, England, 1797/8
OH. $^{5}/_{8}$", OL. $1^{7}/_{16}$", OW. $1^{3}/_{16}$"
L1999-187

90. **Susanna Barker**

London, England, ca. 1790
OH. ⁷/₈", OL. 2³/₁₆", OW. 1⁷/₁₆"
L1999-183

91. **Susanna Barker**

London, England, 1791/2
OH. ⁷/₈", OL. 1¹³/₁₆", OW. 1⁵/₁₆"
L1999-133

92. **George Smith II and Thomas Hayter**
London, 1803/4
OH. 15/16", OL. 1 3/4", OW. 1 3/16"
L1999-188

93. **Probably James Ruell**
London, England, 1812/3
Owners' initials *MAW* in script
engraved on face of cover
OH. 1", OL. 1 9/16", OW. 1"
L1999-149

BIRMINGHAM

1796–1844

*Escalating consumer demand drove the rapid
expansion of Birmingham's metal trades during
the last half of the eighteenth and first half of
the nineteenth centuries. Enterprising entrepreneurs, benefiting from efficient organization and
mechanical assistance, responded to the demand
for small fashion goods with large quantities of
all types, including silver nutmeg graters.*

Back row; middle row; front row; right

94. **Samuel Pemberton**
Birmingham, England, 1796/7
OH. 1 1/16", OL. 1 3/8", OW. 15/16"
L1999-195

95. **Samuel Pemberton**
Birmingham, England, 1791/2
OH. 1 1/16", DIAM. (covers) 15/16"
L1999-166

96. **Samuel Pemberton**
Birmingham, England, 1798/9
OH. 1 15/16"
L1999-153

97. **Samuel Pemberton**
Birmingham, England, 1801/2
OH. 7/8", OL. 1 3/8", OW. 15/16"
L1999-194

98. **Samuel Pemberton**
Birmingham, England, 1792/3
Owner's initials *AS* in script
engraved on top of upper cover
OH. 1 5/16", DIAM. (covers) 7/8"
L1999-176

99. **Samuel Pemberton**
Birmingham, England, 1793/4
OH. 1 1/8", DIAM. (covers) 7/8"
L1999-175

100. **Samuel Pemberton**
Birmingham, England, 1801/2
OH. 13/16", OL. 1 3/8", OW. 7/8"
L1999-196

101. **Samuel Pemberton**
Birmingham, England, 1819/20
OL. 1 3/8", DIAM. (cover) 1"
L1999-150

102. **Samuel Pemberton**
Birmingham, England, 1796/7
Owner's initials *JC* in script
engraved on top of upper cover
OH. 1 1/4", DIAM. (covers) 15/16"
L1999-94

103. **Henry J. Pepper**
Wilmington, Delaware, ca. 1820
Owners' initials *AHP* in script
engraved on face of lower cover
OH. 2", DIAM. (covers) 1 3/16"
L1999-88

Because of its verbatim dependence
on Birmingham models, this Delaware
example is shown with the group. The
grater, like the barrel by Samuel Kirk
(no. 27), is much larger than its English
prototype. Aside from its size, Pepper's
grater is indistinguishable from those
made by Samuel Pemberton.

104. Joseph Taylor

Birmingham, England, 1813/4
Unidentified owner's crest engraved
on face of cover
OH. 1", OL. 1⁹/₁₆", OW. 1⅛"
L1999-92

105. Joseph Taylor

Birmingham, England, 1799/1800
OL. 2¼"
L1999-120

106. Joseph Taylor

Birmingham, England, 1802/3
Owner's initials *CW* in script
engraved on face of cover
OH. ¾", OL. 1⅜", OW. 1"
L1999-186

107. Joseph Taylor

Birmingham, England, 1799/1800
OL. 1¼"
L1999-185

108. Joseph Willmore

Birmingham, England, 1822/3
Owner's initials *J.C.* in gothic letters
engraved on face of cover
OH. ¹⁵/₁₆", OL. 1⁵/₁₆", OW. ¹⁵/₁₆"
L1999-200

109. Joseph Willmore

Birmingham, England, 1810/1
Owner's initials *EN* in script
engraved on face of cover
OH. ⁷/₈", OL. 1⁹/₁₆", OW. 1¹/₁₆"
L1999-172

110. **John Shaw**

Birmingham, England, 1803/4
OH. ⁷/₈", OL. 1¹¹/₁₆", OW. 1³/₁₆"
L1999-193

111. **John Shaw**

Birmingham, England, 1804/5
Owner's initials *TL* in gothic letters
engraved on face of body opposite
hinge
OH. ¹⁵/₁₆", OL. 1¹¹/₁₆", OW. 1³/₁₆"
L1999-134

112. **Thomas Shaw**

Birmingham, England, 1836/7
OH. ¹³/₁₆", OL. 1¹/₂", OW. 1⁵/₁₆"
L1999-198

113. **Nathaniel Mills**

Birmingham, England, 1841/2
Owners' initials *PWH* in script
engraved on face of cover
OH. 1¹/₁₆", OL. 1⁹/₁₆", OW. ¹⁵/₁₆"
L1999-169

114. **Nathaniel Mills**

Birmingham, England, 1847/8
Owners' initials *C.M.G.* in script
engraved on face of cover
OH. 1¹/₁₆", OL. 1⁷/₁₆", OW. 1"
L1999-184

115. **Wheeler & Cronin**
Birmingham, England, 1843/4
Unidentified owner's crest engraved
on face of cover
OH. 1^1/16", OL. 1^{15}/16", OW. 1^9/16"
L1999-128

116. Possibly John Law

Sheffield, England, ca. 1800
OH. $^{15}/_{16}$", OL. $1^{5}/_{8}$", OW. $1^{1}/_{2}$"
L1999-165

SCOTLAND

1825–1896

*Although England and Scotland had been politi-
cally united since the early eighteenth century,
many factors continued to separate them. England
treated Scotland as a foreign country, and the
Scots considered themselves a people apart. They
sought a distinctive appearance in many of their
household and personal possessions. These objects
can be described as nationalistic rather than
merely provincial.*

117. **JK (unidentified)**

Edinburgh, Scotland, ca. 1850
Owner's crest and motto of Monteith
family and the gothic letter *C* engraved
on face of body
OH. 3"
L1999-123

This brilliant example of highly individual form is handsomely engraved
in the rococo revival manner.

118. **James McKay**

Cover inset with agate
Edinburgh, Scotland, ca. 1830
OH. 1", OL. 1½", OW. 1⅜"
L1999-109

119. **Brook & Son Ltd.**

Edinburgh, Scotland, 1895/6
Unidentified owner's crest and motto
engraved on face of body and initials
MT in script engraved on face of cover
OL. 2⅝"
L1999-121

United States

1911–1975

American firms and individual silversmiths continued to produce nutmeg graters in the twentieth century. They drew their inspiration from various sources. Tiffany & Co.'s plain cube assumes a minimalist approach, while William de Matteo's reproduction of an eighteenth-century model reflects his tenure as Colonial Williamsburg's master silversmith.

120. **William de Matteo**

Williamsburg, Virginia, ca. 1970
OH. 1⅛", OL. 1¹⁵⁄₁₆", OW. 1⁷⁄₁₆"
L1999-102

William de Matteo served as silversmith for Colonial Williamsburg from 1953 until 1979. This grater was probably inspired by a mid-eighteenth-century English example in the collections of Colonial Williamsburg (1939-179).

121. **Jenkins & Jenkins**

Baltimore, Maryland, ca. 1911
Owners' initials *A/EP/❋* engraved on face of lower cover and date "20 May 1911" engraved on face of other
OH. 1¹⁄₁₆", OL. 1¾", OW. 1⅛"
L1999-158

122. **Tiffany & Co.**

New York, New York, ca. 1920
Owners' initials *P.C.P.* in script engraved on face
OH. 1³⁄₁₆"
L1999-116

NUTMEG POISONING

Robert C. Green Jr., M.D., Winchester, Va.

Reprinted from The Journal of The American
Medical Association, *November 7, 1959, Vol. 171,
pp. 1342–1344*

Copyrighted 1959, American Medical Association

*From the Medical Service, Community Memorial
Hospital, South Hill, Va.*

The present-day use of nutmeg (Myristica fragrans) *is
confined largely to exploitation of its properties as a fla-
voring agent. In the past it has been used medicinally as
an aromatic stimulant, a carminative, and a narcotic.
In England and India it has been used widely by the laity
as an emmenagogue and an abortifacient, and from these
uses came many reports of nutmeg poisoning in the early
literature. During the last 50 years nutmeg poisoning has
seldom been reported, and only limited information is
available concerning the physiological and biochemical
effects of this particular toxic state.*

Review of the Literature

One of the earliest cases of nutmeg poisoning was
recorded by de Lobel in 1576.[1] In 1832 Purkinje[2]
dramatically illustrated the toxic effect of this kernel
by consuming three nutmegs, producing a narcosis
which progressed to stupor. In 1903 Wallace,[3] in a
review of cases of nutmeg poisoning reported 25 from
the world literature. Although one of the patients concerned died,[4] the remaining 24 recovered promptly
without residual effects. Since Wallace's review a
limited number of cases of nutmeg poisoning have
been noted in the literature.[5] These more recent reports are brief; the clinical descriptions are meager
and laboratory studies are not included. It is apparent from these reports and those of Wallace that
only limited observation of nutmeg poisoning
is available. Therefore, it was felt that a detailed
report of such a case from my experience would
be of interest.

Report of a Case

A 28-year-old woman was admitted to the Community Memorial Hospital in South Hill, Va., in a semistuporous condition. The medical and psychiatric
history up to this time had been normal. She had
been married nine years and had experienced two un-
eventful pregnancies. At 10 P.M. on the night before
admission to the hospital she had eaten 18.3 Gm. of
finely ground nutmeg in an attempt to induce the
menses, which had been delayed two days. She had
slept soundly without disturbance until 5:30 A.M. the
next day. At that time she had been awakened by a
burning sensation in the lower part of the abdomen
and an overwhelming feeling of impending death. She

vomited once. Her legs felt as if they were asleep and she complained of feeling "funny all over." She had then become completely disoriented, with episodes of wild screaming and purposeless thrashing of the arms and legs. Coordination appeared absent. Interspersed with this disorientation were brief moments of lucidity during which she seemed to be aware of her surroundings. From the time of her awakening at 5:30 A.M. until 9:30 A.M., when she was seen by her local physician, there were three intervals of lucidity, each lasting about 10 minutes. The rest of this time she was delirious and in a state of excitement and agitation.

This patient was admitted to the hospital at 11:30 A.M., about 13 hours after she had taken the nutmeg. On admission she was in a semistupor. She could be aroused to talk, but would immediately return to the semistuporous condition. The skin was cool but not clammy. There was no cyanosis. Blood pressure initially was 100/50 mm. Hg, pulse rate 100 and respirations 24 per minute, and temperature 98 F (36.7 C). The pupils were small and reaction to light was not visible. The thorax was clear to auscultation, palpation, and percussion. The heart was not enlarged and there were no murmurs. The abdomen was not tender and the liver, spleen, and kidneys were not palpable. The extremity reflexes were absent. Pelvic examination revealed evidence of beginning menstrual flow. Results of rectal examination were negative. The erythrocyte count was 3,710,000 per cubic millimeter, and the hemoglobin value was 6.8 Gm. per 100 cc. The leukocyte count was 7,400 per cubic millimeter, with 87% segmented neutrophils and 13% lymphocytes. Results of serologic tests were negative. Specific gravity of the urine was 1.020;

the hydrogen-ion concentration was acid. Albumin content of urine was graded 2+; there was neither sugar nor bile. The carbon dioxide-combining power was 14.9 mEq. per liter of plasma. The serum sodium content was 126 mEq. per liter and plasma chloride content, 108 mEq. per liter. The serum potassium concentration was 3.8 mEq. per liter. The value for serum nonprotein nitrogen was 47 mg. per 100 cc.

The patient remained in a semistupor for 12 hours after her admission. She then began to experience episodes of wild excitement, with loud screaming and manifestations of a fear of impending death. She continued to be subjected to episodes of excitement for two hours, during which time restraints were needed. For the remainder of the second day she was restless but essentially quiet. During the third and fourth days of hospitalization she slept much but complained constantly, while awake, of a generalized feeling of numbness and dizziness.

Laboratory investigation on the third day revealed the value for serum nonprotein nitrogen to be 36.5 mg. per 100 cc. The specific gravity of the urine was 1.020; the hydrogen-ion concentration was acid. There was no albumin, sugar, or bile in the urine. The result of the sulfobromophthalein tolerance test was 10.5% retention of dye in 30 minutes. The direct serum bilirubin content was 0.05 mg. per 100 cc.; total bilirubin was 0.35 mg. per 100 cc. The reaction of the cephalin flocculation test was graded negative. On the fourth day of hospitalization the result of a phenolsulfonphthalein test was recorded as 77% excretion of the dye in two hours. Urine obtained during this test had a specific gravity of 1.002; there was no sugar, albumin, or bile. Total serum proteins amounted to

6.1 Gm. per 100 cc., with 4.5 Gm. of albumin and
1.6 Gm. of globulin. The prothrombin time was recorded as 100%. A transthoracic procedure to obtain
hepatic tissue for biopsy was done at this time. Micro-
scopic sections of the tissue showed no evidence of
fatty infiltration or hepatic cell necrosis.

On the fifth hospital day the patient complained
of nausea, dizziness, and generalized numbness. At
intervals throughout this day she became restless and
noisy and frequently expressed a fear of imminent
death. These symptoms persisted intermittently with
decreasing frequency and intensity through the sixth
day. Between these episodes she appeared essentially
normal.

She was discharged on the seventh hospital day.
Laboratory studies at that time revealed retention of
sulfobromophthalein to be 8% in 30 minutes. The
specific gravity of the urine was 1.024; there was a
trace of albumin, but no sugar or bile. The hydrogen-
ion concentration was acid. The direct serum bilirubin content was 0.15 mg. per 100 cc., and the total
bilirubin was 0.95 per 100 cc.

The patient returned for follow-up studies 10 days
after discharge. At that time the results obtained from
a complete blood cell count; urinalysis; cephalin flocculation, sulfobromophthalein, and serum bilirubin
tests; and determination of nonprotein nitrogen remained essentially unchanged from those recorded at
previous procedures. She reported that she was without symptoms of any kind. Because of the limited
information available concerning nutmeg poisoning
no specific therapy was given in this case, except for
intramuscular injections of promazine hydrochloride
during periods of excitement.

Comment

On the basis of the data in this case and in those
noted from the literature it is apparent that nutmeg
taken in moderate quantities may produce a serious
toxic state and possibly death. To obtain a clearer
understanding of the problem the pharmacological
and chemical features of nutmeg will be discussed,
as well as the clinical syndrome resulting from ingestion of the substance in toxic amounts. Because
of the almost total absence of interest in this subject
in the recent literature all information concerning
the properties of nutmeg have come from a limited
number of early studies.

Pharmacological Aspects—Wallace reported that
the toxic factor of nutmeg is confined entirely to
the volatile oil component. He administered this
oil (0.4 grains [24 mg.] per kilogram of body weight)
to cats by a stomach tube and produced a striking
clinical response. Within 10 minutes he noted restlessness, excitement, and excessive salivation. These
signs were followed by a period of quiet associated with
incoordination and staggering. Mydriasis was usually
noted at this time. The reflexes became weakened and
a condition of semiconsciousness supervened, during
which respiration became labored and feeble. In some
animals unconsciousness deepened, respiration became labored and feeble, and death occurred 8 to
12 hours after ingestion of the oil. Usually, however,
after the stage of unconsciousness had developed,
gradual improvement occurred, and at about 15 hours
after the oil had been given the animal appeared to
return to normal. This improvement generally was
temporary; the animal then gradually weakened, and
within 36 to 72 hours after administration of the oil

coma developed and death followed. Autopsy of these animals consistently showed advanced fatty degeneration of the liver.

Dale[6] and Jurss,[7] with use of myristicin, a constituent of the volatile oil, were able to reproduce in animals symptoms identical to those caused by the administration of nutmeg or the volatile oil of nutmeg. They concluded that myristicin is the toxic factor in nutmeg. Autopsy of their animals showed changes in the liver similar to those described by Wallace.

Chemical Aspects—Nutmeg is known to contain from 5 to 15% volatile oil, 25 to 40% fixed oil, and 5 to 15% ash. The rest is starch, fiber, and water.[8] Power and Solway,[9] in an analysis of this volatile oil, found that 4% was myristicin. The formula for myristicin is $C_{11}H_{12}O_3$, and it is 5-allyl-1-methoxy-2,3, methylene-dioxybenzene. Further analysis of the volatile oil revealed 80% to be dextrocamphene and dextropinene, with 8% dipentene. Also noted were small amounts of eugenol, iso-eugenol, linalool, borneol, terpineol, geraniol, and safrol. In addition, Power and Solway isolated limited amounts of free myristic acid and traces of esters of this and other fatty acids.

Clinical Aspects—It is apparent from this case and those previously reported that nutmeg in doses of 5 Gm. or more will produce a characteristic clinical syndrome. From one to seven hours after the ingestion of nutmeg symptoms of a burning midabdominal pain, with or without vomiting, may occur. Restlessness, giddiness, and excitement may be noted. Frequently a fear of impending death is reported, and often there is the complaint of a sensation of a heavy weight on the chest. During the next 10 hours drowsiness progressing to stupor may develop. However,

the patient can be aroused; if this is done, delirium and agitation ensue and the patient sinks again into stupor. Some patients may not manifest the early symptoms of toxicity but may display only the late narcotic effect. As a rule recovery is complete within 24 hours. However, large doses of nutmeg may prolong recovery, and periodic outbursts of excitement with delirium may continue for several days or more.

Significant physical findings may include a decrease in blood pressure, with cyanosis and shock. In addition, there may be rapid respiration, tachycardia, dilatation of the pupils, and decreased or absent peripheral reflexes. Several of the early reports suggest that some patients may exhibit, in addition to the usual symptoms and signs, an acute allergic response to nutmeg. This response is manifested by edema of the eyelids, with marked flushing and itching of the face. There also may be an elevation of temperature. These symptoms of an allergic reaction apparently subside quickly.

Some of the laboratory findings in the case I have reported are not entirely understood. Since previous studies did not contain laboratory reports, the chemical determinations recorded in the present case are difficult to evaluate. In this case acidosis was noted, with depression of the values for serum sodium and serum potassium. The serum chloride content was within the normal range.

On the basis of the experimental work on cats by Wallace, Dale, and Jurss it appeared that fatty degeneration of the liver was the end-result of toxic doses of the volatile oil or its derivative myristicin. However, in the case reported here serial studies of hepatic function as well as biopsy of tissue from the liver revealed no evidence of damage to that structure.

Studies of renal function revealed an initial slight elevation of the nonprotein nitrogen value, as well as albumin content of grade 2+, although the output of urine during the first 24 hours was normal. The value for nonprotein nitrogen returned to normal the next day, and a subsequent urinalysis disclosed occasional traces of albumin. It seems probable that in the case presented here nutmeg produced a transient toxic effect on the kidney.

Summary

The toxic factor of nutmeg is known to be myristicin, a constituent of the volatile oil of nutmeg. Nutmeg in doses of 5 Gm. or more produces a marked depressive action on the central nervous system, as well as a less prominent stimulating effect. The clinical course may be severe, with coma, shock, and acidosis as its main features.

117 W. Boscawen St.

References

1. De Lobel, M.: Plantarum sev stirpium historia, Antwerp, Christopher Plantin Architypograph, 1576, p. 570.

2. Ueber die narkotische Wirkung der Muskatnuss, in Purkinje, J. E.: Einige Beiträge zur physiologischen Pharmacologie: Neue Breslauer Sammlungen aus dem Gebiete der Heilkunde, Breslau, im Verlage von H. Gosohorsky, 1829, vol. 1, pp. 423–444.

3. Wallace, G. B.: On Nutmeg Poisoning, Contrib. Med. Research (Vaughan), Ann Arbor, Mich., pp. 351–364, 1903.

4. Dodge, W. T.: Nutmeg Poisoning, Med. Rec. N.Y. **32**:624, 1887.

5. Bartlett, B. F.: Nutmeg Poisoning, Brit. M. J. **2**:269, 1911. Hamond, P. W.: Nutmeg Poisoning, ibid. **2**:788, 1906. Hamilton, J.: Nutmeg Poisoning, ibid. **2**:900, 1906. Wilkinson, A. N.: Poisoning by Nutmeg, ibid. **1**:539, 1906. Johnson, J.: Nutmeg Poisoning, ibid. **2**:984, 1906. Gibbins, K. M.: Nutmeg Poisoning, ibid. **1**:1005, 1909. Pitter, R. A.: Case of Nutmeg Poisoning, Lancet **1**:1035, 1902. Reekie, J. S.: Nutmeg Poisoning, J. A. M. A. **2**:62, 1909.

6. Dale, H. H.: Note on Nutmeg Poisoning, Proc. Roy. Soc. Med. **2**:69–74, 1908–1909.

7. Jurss, F.: On Myristicin and Some Closely Related Substances: Bericht of Schimmel and Co. Leipzig, Germany, (April) 1904, pp. 159–165.

8. Dispensatory of United States of America, ed. 25, Philadelphia, J. B. Lippincott Company, 1955, pp. 873–875.

9. Power, B. F., and Solway, A. H.: Constituents of Essential Oil of Nutmeg, Trans. Chem. Soc. London **91** (pt. 2): 2037–2057, 1907.

BIBLIOGRAPHY

Delieb, Eric. *Investing in Silver.* New York, N.Y.: Clarkson N. Potter, 1967.

Helliwell, Stephen. *Collecting Small Silverware.* Oxford, England: Phaidon-Christie's, 1988.

Hughes, George Bernard. *Small Antique Silverware.* London, England: B.T. Batsford, 1957.

Hughes, George Bernard. "Silver Nutmeg-Graters." *Country Life* CXVI (1954), pp. 2306–2307.

Miles, Elizabeth B. *The English Silver Pocket Nutmeg Grater: A Collection of Fifty Examples from 1693 to 1816.* Cleveland, Ohio: C.W. Printing Service, 1966.

Ransome-Wallis, Rosemary. *Matthew Boulton and the Toymakers: Silver from the Birmingham Assay Office.* London, England: The Worshipful Company of Goldsmiths, 1982.

Smith, Guy Oswald. "Silver Nutmeg Graters or Spice Boxes." *Connoisseur* XIX (1907), pp. 169–173.

Index of Makers

Listed by catalog number